ALL NEW EDITION ✳ NICK HARPER

TOP 10 FOR
MEN

OVER 200 MORE
MANLY LISTS!

hamlyn

An Hachette UK Company
www.hachette.co.uk

First published in Great Britain in 2014 by
Hamlyn, a division of Octopus Publishing Group Ltd
Endeavour House
189 Shaftesbury Avenue
London
WC2H 8JY
www.octopusbooks.co.uk

ISBN 978-0-600-62916-0

A CIP catalogue record for this book is available from the British Library

Printed and bound by CPI Group (UK) Ltd, Croydon, CR0 4YY

10 9 8 7 6 5 4 3 2 1

Editorial Director: Trevor Davies
Project Editor: Clare Churly
Art Director: Jonathan Christie
Designer and illustrator: Jeremy Tilston
Senior Production Manager: Peter Hunt

Contents

Music

Celebrities

Technology

Names

Sex

Life & Death

Transport

Sport

History

Miscellaneous

Introduction

It's 1998, the first day of my first proper job. A man I'd only just met asked me to list the 10 greatest films ever made. I was caught off guard. I tried to remember what I'd seen. 'Erm, *Pulp Fiction... The Godfather... Part II...* er... *LA Confidential*?'

As I stammered, he frowned. 'Every man needs his top 10s,' he said. 'His 10 greatest films, albums, cars, footballers, newsreaders – you can tell everything about a man by his lists.'

I thought my new colleague had too much time on his hands, and he probably did, but when I returned to my desk and started working out my top 10 films, I realized he was right.

Most men live their lives by their lists. We might not mean to but we do. The greatest albums ever made? The best cities on the planet? The classic flavours of crisps? They're all lodged in your brain, waiting to be listed, because at some point, someone will want to know. It won't ever be a woman. Women love lists too, but their lists tend to cover the vital stuff that keeps the world turning, allowing us to sit back and ponder computer games and cheese.

The remarkable thing about lists is their ability to unite people with seemingly nothing in common. Ask the Prime Minister for his 10 favourite sandwich fillings and his list would be no more important than that of a man who sweeps the streets for a living.

That's because the list is one of life's great levellers. And because of that, lists help complete strangers find common ground. I was once introduced to a bloke at a barbecue who answered my every question with a 'Yes' or a 'No' and an awkward silence. By now I had my former colleague's advice embedded in my mind so I cleverly steered him onto the subject of music, then asked for his top 10 albums. He rattled them out in no time, in order and in great detail, and the ice was broken.

Now I only mention this because last summer I was asked by a different man if I'd be interested in compiling a book of lists. My first thought was that he hadn't been able to track down my former colleague so he'd opted for me instead. My second thought was that I'd better get cracking, because a book containing this many lists would take some work. And indeed it did. But six months later the book was complete and absolutely creaking with top 10s on every subject imaginable.

Some of the lists are based on hard, irrefutable fact, the rest are more subjective and open to argument. But what unites each and every one is the desire to inform and entertain. These lists will arm you with knowledge to carry around in your head, just waiting for that moment when somebody casually asks you to name your top 10 this or that. Because they will, and because it's true: every man needs his lists.

(Speaking of which, Rob, sorry this has taken so long.)

The 10 greatest films ever made, according to me:

1 *Carlito's Way*

2 *Dazed and Confused*

3 *Pulp Fiction*

4 *This Is Spinal Tap*

5 *Grosse Pointe Blank*

6 *Casino*

7 *Pan's Labyrinth*

8 *Boogie Nights*

9 *Tell No One*

10 *The Empire Strikes Back*

Top 10 greatest films of all time*

FILM/YEAR/DIRECTOR/STARRING	AVERAGE SCORE[†]

1 *The Shawshank Redemption* (1994) Director: Frank Darabont. Starring: Tim Robbins, Morgan Freeman. — 9.2

2 *The Godfather* (1972) Director: Francis Ford Coppola. Starring: Al Pacino, Marlon Brando, James Caan. — 9.2

3 *The Godfather: Part II* (1974) Director: Francis Ford Coppola. Starring: Al Pacino, Robert De Niro, Robert Duvall. — 9

4 *Pulp Fiction* (1994) Director: Quentin Tarantino. Starring: John Travolta, Bruce Willis, Samuel L. Jackson, Uma Thurman. — 8.9

5 *The Good, the Bad and the Ugly* (1966) Director: Sergio Leone. Starring: Clint Eastwood, Eli Wallach, Lee Van Cleef. — 8.9

6 *The Dark Knight* (2008) Director: Christopher Nolan. Starring: Christian Bale, Heath Ledger, Aaron Eckhart. — 8.9

7 *12 Angry Men* (1957) Director: Sidney Lumet. Starring: Henry Fonda, Lee J. Cobb, Martin Balsam. — 8.9

8 *Schindler's List* (1993) Director: Steven Spielberg. Starring: Liam Neeson, Ralph Fiennes, Ben Kingsley. — 8.9

9 *The Lord of the Rings: The Return of the King* (2003) Director: Peter Jackson. Starring: Elijah Wood, Viggo Mortensen, Ian McKellen. — 8.8

10 *Fight Club* (1999) Director: David Fincher. Starring: Brad Pitt, Ed Norton, Helena Bonham Carter. — 8.8

*As ranked by Internet Movie Database (IMDb) regular users as at October 2013

[†]Average scores are out of 10. Where ratings scores are equal, films with more votes rank higher

Source: 'IMDb's Top 10 Greatest Films of All Time', www.imdb.com

Top 10 critically acclaimed films*

FILM/YEAR	METASCORE†	AVERAGE USER SCORE‡
1 ***The Godfather*** (1972)	100	8.9
2 ***Lawrence of Arabia*** (1962; re-released 2002)	100	8.5
3 ***The Wizard of Oz*** (1939)	100	8.1
=4 ***The Leopard*** (1963; re-released 2004)	100	7.9
=4 ***Fanny and Alexander*** (1982; re-released 2004)	100	7.9
6 ***The Conformist*** (1970; re-released 2005)	100	7.5
7 ***Balthazar*** (1966; re-released 2003)	100	7
8 ***Sweet Smell of Success*** (1957; re-released 2002)	100	6.6
9 ***Best Kept Secret*** (2013)	100	6.3
10 ***Voyage to Italy*** (1954; re-released 2013)	100	4.3

*According to online review aggregator Metacritic

†Each film in this list has received a Metascore of 100 (the highest possible score). The Metascore is a weighted average of published critics' reviews as calculated by Metacritic

‡Ranked by Metacritic's user scores (out of 10) as at November 2013

Source: Metacritic, www.metacritic.com

Top 10 greatest Hollywood actors of all time*

ACTOR	'BEST ACTOR' WINS	NOMINATIONS†
❶ Daniel Day-Lewis	3	5
❷ Jack Nicholson‡	2	12
❸ Spencer Tracy	2	9
❹ Marlon Brando	2	8
❺ Dustin Hoffman	2	7
❻ Sean Penn	2	5 (54 films)
❼ Tom Hanks	2	5 (73 films)
❽ Fredric March	2	5 (85 films)
❾ Gary Cooper	2	5 (118 films)
❿ Laurence Olivier	1	10

*Ranked by the number of Best Actor Academy Award (Oscar) wins as at August 2013. Where equal, actors are ranked by number of Oscar nominations. Where the number of wins and nominations is equal, the actor with fewer films receives a higher position.

†In the Best Actor and Best Supporting Actor categories

‡Nicholson has also won an Oscar for Best Supporting Actor

Source: Film totals are based on Internet Movie Database (IMDb) statistics, www.imdb.com

Top 10 most 'valuable' actors of all time*

ACTOR	TOTAL FILMS	TOTAL US BOX OFFICE GROSS	AVERAGE US BOX OFFICE GROSS	OSCAR WINS
1 Tom Hanks	40	$6.2 billion	$155.4 million	2
2 Harrison Ford	34	$7.4 billion	$218.3 million	0
3 Eddie Murphy	38	$5.9 billion	$154.6 million	0
4 Robin Williams	44	$4.8 billion	$108.4 million	1
5 Tom Cruise	33	$5 billion	$153 million	0
6 Dustin Hoffman	39	$4.6 billion	$117.5 million	2
7 Sean Connery	37	$4.5 billion	$122.9 million	1
8 Morgan Freeman	47	$4.5 billion	$95.8 million	1
9 Clint Eastwood	46	$4.3 billion	$93.3 million	0
10 John Travolta	43	$4.3 billion	$99.7 million	0

*Based on a ranking of actors by 24/7 Wall St. (see note below). Figures correct as at January 2013

Source: 24/7 Wall St., www.247wallst.com

24/7 Wall St. ranked nearly 700 leading actors in Box Office Mojo's database. Actors ranked higher if they starred in more films, if the films they starred in averaged high ticket sales, and if they had among the highest combined box office gross adjusted for ticket price inflation. This last component was weighted more heavily. All film gross numbers are based on US ticket sales only, and, unless otherwise noted, are adjusted for ticket price inflation, as calculated by Box Office Mojo. Awards, such as Oscar wins and nominations, came from the Internet Movie Database (IMDb).

10 controversial films

1 *The Wild One* (1953) – A tale of a motorcycle gang wreaking havoc in small-town America, the Marlon Brando vehicle was denied a UK release amid fears it would lead to social unrest. When finally released in 1967, the PG certificate reflected the film's relatively timid content.

2 *The Texas Chainsaw Massacre* (1974) – A violent tale of a group of friends kidnapped and murdered by a disfigured redneck, released but quickly banned in the UK until 1999 – having been resubmitted to the British Board of Film Classification (BBFC) to mark its 25th anniversary.

3 *A Clockwork Orange* (1971) – Not banned, as many believe, but withdrawn by Stanley Kubrick between 1973 and 2000 due to death threats against the director and his family. The 'ban' was lifted following his death in 1999.

4 *Enter the Dragon* (1973) – The Bruce Lee classic was never banned but heavily cut amid the BBFC's concerns that the heavily stylized martial arts would lead youngsters astray – all flying stars and nunchuks were removed from the film.

5 *Natural Born Killers* (1994) – Amid fears of copycat killings, the BBFC sat on Oliver Stone's tale of serial-killers-made-celebrities for six months before finally passing it for a theatrical release in February 1995.

6 *Monty Python's Life of Brian* (1979) – The comic tale of Brian, a regular man mistaken for the Messiah and crucified in singsong, was considered too blasphemous for release by 39 UK councils. Many backed down but Glasgow maintained its ban for 30 years.

7 *Straw Dogs* (1971) – Banned for containing a four-minute rape scene that appeared to endorse or eroticize sexual violence. Clinical psychologists advised the BBFC before its ban was finally lifted and the film was released uncut.

8 *The Exorcist* (1974) – One of horror's most controversial releases, *The Exorcist* fell foul of the Video Recordings Act and, despite being passed for cinema release by the BBFC in 1974, was denied a video release that remained in place until 1999.

9 *Deep Throat* (1972) – Pioneering porn film that saw charges of obscenity in several cities across the USA. In the UK, the film was banned by the BBFC and not passed uncut until 2000, when it received an 18 certificate DVD release.

10 *Reservoir Dogs* (1992) – Quentin Tarantino's debut was never officially banned from a home video release in the UK, but denied a classification amid hysteria over film violence. It didn't surface on VHS for three years, by which point *Pulp Fiction* and the Tarantino-penned *True Romance* had both been released.

10 most unlikely murder weapons in film history

FILM

1 **A television** – In *Grosse Pointe Blank*, hitman Martin Q. Blank ends a shoot-out by slamming a large, old-style television over the head of rival hitman, Grocer, killing him instantly.

2 **A giant plaster penis** – In the infamous *A Clockwork Orange*, Alex DeLarge beats the owner of the house he's broken into with a weapon from her own collection of erotic art. The final blows are delivered by an oversized plaster penis.

3 **A bowling ball** – In *There Will Be Blood*, Daniel Plainview beats Eli Sunday to death during the demented denouement. The film's title hinted at bloodshed, but Plainview's weapon of choice – a bowling ball – came as quite the surprise.

4 **A can of hairspray** – In *True Romance*, a hitman played by James Gandolfini meets a grisly end when inventive hooker Alabama sets his head on fire using a flame and a can of hairspray – having already stuck a corkscrew in his foot and hit him over the head with the top of a cistern.

5 **A steak** – In *Law Abiding Citizen*, having demanded and then devoured a porterhouse steak, Clyde Shelton uses the steak's bone to brutally murder his unsuspecting cellmate, stabbing him several times in the neck until he's absolutely and utterly dead.

6 **A trident** – In *Anchorman: The Legend of Ron Burgundy*, Brick Tamland brags he 'killed a guy with a trident'. Though we never see it, 'there were horses, and a man on fire', and he stabbed a man in the heart with a three-pronged spear. 'You're probably wanted for murder,' warns Burgundy.

7 **A pencil** – In *The Dark Knight*, The Joker entertains a room full of mob muscle with a magic trick, making a pencil disappear by impaling it in the head of an unsuspecting victim – entering through what looks to be his eyeball.

8 **A carrot** – In *Shoot 'Em Up*, in the most striking of a series of assaults using the humble carrot, the lead protagonist Smith inserts the vegetable into the mouth of one poor bad guy before punching it clean through the back of his throat. Why a carrot? Why not?

9 **Food** – In *Se7en*, starring Brad Pitt and Morgan Freeman, the villainous John Doe force-feeds one of his victims to his gut-busting death. In doing so he ticks the box marked 'gluttony' in the seven deadly sins.

10 **A giant rubber dildo** – In *Lock, Stock and Two Smoking Barrels*, underworld boss Hatchet Harry beats an associate to death using the first thing to hand. Which happens to be a massive black rubber cock.

10 films filled with the word 'f**k!'

FILM/YEAR	ESTIMATED TOTAL MENTIONS*	FILM LENGTH	RATE
1 *Nil by Mouth* (1997)	522	128 minutes	4.07 per minute
2 *Alpha Dog* (2007)	411	122 minutes	3.36 per minute
3 *Twin Town* (1997)	318	99 minutes	3.21 per minute
4 *Menace II Society* (1993)	300	97 minutes	3.09 per minute
5 *End of Watch* (2012)	326	109 minutes	2.99 per minute
6 *Narc* (2002)	298	105 minutes	2.83 per minute
7 *Harsh Times* (2006)	296	105 minutes	2.81 per minute
8 *Casino* (1995)	428	178 minutes	2.4 per minute
9 *Summer of Sam* (1999)	326	142 minutes	2.29 per minute
10 *Goodfellas* (1990)	296	146 minutes	2.02 per minute

*Including variations of the F-word. Sadly, no definitive word count exists; figures listed here are as accurate as information allows

These are among the most expletive-riddled films ever made but this cannot be considered a definitive Top 10. Films such as *Gutterballs* and *Mutilation Mile* both have higher F-bomb counts, but they barely pricked the public consciousness as films so find no place here.

10 deadly film killers

1 **Ogami Itto** (*Lone Wolf and Cub: White Heaven in Hell*, 1974) – Top of this list for the simple fact that Itto slayed 150 inside 83 minutes.

2 **Jules Winfield** (*Pulp Fiction*, 1994) – Far from Hollywood's hardest-working hitman – just three kills in all 154 minutes – but with Samuel L. Jackson's Winfield, it's style over substance.

3 **Léon** (*Léon: The Professional*, 1994) – The Jean Reno hitman opened his door and life to 12-year-old neighbour Mathilda, whose family had been slayed by corrupt NYC DEA. What followed was a masterclass in the art of 'cleaning'.

4 **Nikita** (*Nikita*, 1990) – The deadliest reformed junkie in film history, Anne Parillaud is a killer of rare and truly terrifying ruthlessness.

5 **Vincent** (*Collateral*, 2004) – Largely on this list because who knew Hollywood heartthrob Tom Cruise had it in him to play such a terrifyingly single-minded and sociopathic killer?

6 **Angel Eyes** (*The Good, the Bad and the Ugly*, 1966) – Cold-eyed Lee Van Cleef created the Western's most iconic villain, a ruthless, unrelenting hired gun you couldn't help but root for.

7 **The Bride** (*Kill Bill Vol. 1* and *Vol. 2*, 2003 and 2004) – Uma Thurman's Bride slayed 76 in *Kill Bill Vol. 1*, just to reach her true target, the titular Bill – her only kill in *Vol. 2*.

8 **Smith** (*Shoot 'Em Up*, 2007) – Clive Owen's trigger-happy Mr Smith killed 141 in 86 minutes, including some very impressive carrot kills.

9 **Ghost Dog** (*Ghost Dog: The Way of the Samurai*, 1999) – Because there really aren't enough samurai-studying, katana-wielding, meditating pigeon-fanciers in the history of hired hitmen.

10 **Martin Q. Blank** (*Grosse Pointe Blank*, 1997) – John Cusack's gun-for-hire is dark, disillusioned but impressively deadly. A killer of great invention, he killed the President of Paraguay with a fork.

10 of James Bond's greatest gadgets

1 **Shark-inflating pellet** (*Live and Let Die*, 1973) – Pellets designed to expel highly pressurized air to make the target – sharks – explode Used to greater effect when Roger Moore's Bond blew the villainous Dr Kananga to Kingdom Come.

2 **Car invisibility cloak** (*Die Another Day*, 2002) – Pierce Brosnan's Bond had the benefit of a car that couldn't be seen, in this case an Aston Martin Vanquish that became even more desirable when you couldn't see it.

3 **Ericsson phone** (*Tomorrow Never Dies*, 1997) – No one had mobile phones back in 1997, let alone one that could pick locks, scan fingerprints and double as a stun gun. Nowadays there's an app for all of those things, but back in 1997, holy shit!

4 **Seagull snorkel suit** (*Goldfinger*, 1964) – Essential in the arsenal of any agent attempting to infiltrate an enemy facility: a wetsuit with a throw-off-the-scent duck on top of the head, under which 007 dons a perfectly dry, crisp, white, peg-fresh tuxedo with a red carnation.

5 **Briefcase** (*From Russia With Love*, 1963) – The ultimate case for taking care of business. It contained a folding rifle with infrared telescope, 20 concealed rounds of ammunition, a throwing knife and 20 gold sovereigns, plus a tear gas cartridge disguised as talcum powder, set to discharge if the briefcase is opened incorrectly.

6 **Dagger shoe** (*From Russia With Love*, 1963) – Not one of Bond's but one belonging to the delightful SPECTRE agent Rosa Klebb; and one 007 no doubt admired. Klebb's pointy shoes were regulation issue, but with a poison-tipped blade in the toe. One kick could prove fatal, though Bond evaded it.

7 **Omega Seamaster Professional watch** (*GoldenEye*, 1995) – On top of being able to tell the time, Bond's bespoke Omega came with a built-in laser that made cutting through the floor of a train as easy as opening a can of cat food.

8 **Aston Martin DB5** (*Goldfinger*, 1964, and *Thunderball*, 1965) – Like any other car, just with machine gun headlights, oil slick-spraying rear lights, revolving licence plates for evasion, spinning tyre-slasher hubcaps for combat and bulletproof shield for protection. Oh, and a passenger seat ejector for ending conversations.

9 **Bell-Trexton jetpack** (*Thunderball*, 1965) – Though admittedly ludicrous, the sight of Sean Connery's Bond escaping a French château packed full of gun-toting bad sorts by activating a jetpack remains one of the enduring moments in 007 history. When we finally reach The Future, we'll all have them.

10 **Crocodile vessel** (*Octopussy*, 1983) – Taking the seagull snorkel suit of *Goldfinger* a step further, Roger Moore's 007 was able to float his way on to Octopussy's villainous island inside a motorboat disguised as a crocodile.

Top 10 greatest film villains*

CHARACTER	FILM/YEAR	ACTOR

1 The Joker — *The Dark Knight* (2008) — Heath Ledger

'A rare example of a villain who isn't hell bent on world domination, or even personal gain. He just wants to watch the world burn, which makes him so much more terrifying.'

2 Darth Vader — *Star Wars: The Original Trilogy* (1977–83) — David Prowse and James Earl Jones (voice)

'A wheezing, black clad embodiment of evil, Vader casts an impossibly long shadow over the galaxy far, far away and the world of movie villainy in general.'

3 Hannibal Lecter — *The Silence of the Lambs* (1991), *Hannibal* (2001) and *Red Dragon* (2002) — Anthony Hopkins

'A wheedling, taunting mastermind who likes nothing more than the taste of human flesh. Except for messing with the heads of the FBI that is.'

4 Anton Chigurh — *No Country for Old Men* (2007) — Javier Bardem

'A psychotic gun-for-hire with a slavish devotion to the laws of chance. There's nothing more terrifying than a nutcase with a code.'

5 Nurse Ratched — *One Flew Over the Cuckoo's Nest* (1975) — Louise Fletcher

'If you ever found yourself in the unhappy circumstance of placing a relative in a mental institution, you'd hope the staff would show a little more compassion than the demonic Nurse Ratched. The most loathsome embodiment of The Man ever seen on the big screen.'

6 **Jack Torrance**   *The Shining* (1980)   Jack Nicholson
'Contrary to the more sympathetic character found in Stephen King's novel, Kubrick's Torrance seems thoroughly sick of his wife and child even before the Overlook starts to exert its evil influence. Although Shelley Winters' constant shrieking would be enough to drive anyone to axe-murder.'

7 **Amon Goeth**   *Schindler's List* (1993)   Ralph Fiennes
'Fiennes is a revelation as the cold and callous death camp commandant who appears entirely psychotic in his inability to empathize with the inmates under his jurisdiction. A terrifying reminder of the startling inhumanity of the Nazi regime.'

8 **Mr Potter**   *It's a Wonderful Life* (1946)   Lionel Barrymore
'One of the few villains on this list who gets away with his dirty deeds scot-free, Potter really is an unrelenting shit.'

9 **Agent Smith**   *The Matrix* trilogy (1999–2003)   Hugo Weaving
'The nastiest piece of software you could ever hope to come across. His general loathing of humankind makes us want to chuck our laptop in the skip for fear of it going rogue.'

10 **Norman Bates**   *Psycho* (1960)   Anthony Perkins
'A profoundly messed-up young man who not only murdered his mother, but decided to adopt her personality as penance. He loves his dear old mum. If killing her, preserving her corpse and wearing her clothes can be described as love.'

*According to *Total Film*

Source and quotes: *Total Film*, www.totalfilm.com

10 real criminals on whom film gangsters are based

1 **Frank Lawrence 'Lefty' Rosenthal** – A professional sports bettor, former Las Vegas casino executive and organized crime associate. Played by Robert De Niro in *Casino*. In the film, Rosenthal narrowly escaped a mob hit and is last seen in San Diego, working as a sports handicapper for the mob. In real life, banned from Vegas, he ended up in Miami Beach as a sports betting consultant and died of natural causes, aged 79.

2 **Tony 'The Ant' Spilotro** – Mob enforcer in Chicago and Las Vegas. Played by Joe Pesci in *Casino*, though his name was changed to Nicholas 'Nicky' Santoro. In the film, Santoro was brutally beaten and buried alive with his brother in a cornfield. In reality, exact details are unclear but he was either beaten to death in a cornfield or in the basement of a building in Illinois. But in both film and life, he had become a hot-headed liability to the mob.

3 **Thomas DeSimone** – Real-life Lucchese crime family associate in New York. Played by Joe Pesci in *Goodfellas*, his name changed to Tommy DeVito. In the film, DeVito is killed for the murder of a 'made' man, Billy Bats, lured to his death on the pretext of becoming a made man himself. The real DeSimone was allegedly 'whacked' in similar circumstances to those portrayed in the film.

4 **Benjamin Ruggiero** – A foot soldier in New York's Bonanno crime family, the man hoodwinked into allowing Donnie Brasco to infiltrate the mob. Played by Al Pacino in *Donnie Brasco*, in the film's conclusion, once the truth emerges, Ruggiero is summoned to his off-screen death. In reality, Ruggiero was picked up by police en route to what was said to be his own execution and spent time in jail before dying of cancer in 1994, aged 68.

5 **Henry Hill** – New York City mobster and Lucchese family associate. Played by Ray Liotta in *Goodfellas*. In the film he entered witness protection and ended up 'an average nobody'. In real life, he entered witness protection, became 'an average nobody', then a media celebrity, and died aged 69 in 2002 from complications following a heart attack.

6 **Frank Lucas** – Harlem crime boss and very organized drug trafficker. Played by Denzel Washington in *American Gangster*. In the film, Lucas is arrested following the discovery of his heroin HQ and sentenced to 22 years in prison. In reality, sentenced to 70 years in 1976, Lucas cut a deal that reduced it to time served plus lifetime parole. He received a seven-year sentence in 1984, was released in 1991 and remains alive and free to this day.

7 **Dominick 'Sonny Black' Napolitano** – New York Bonanno family 'capo'. Played by Michael Madsen in *Donnie Brasco*. In the film, Napolitano steps into the background as Benjamin Ruggiero's demise takes centre stage (see No. 4). In reality, Napolitano met the end Ruggiero was shown to have in the film – summoned to his death by the mob and shot to death in a Brooklyn basement as punishment for allowing Donnie Brasco to infiltrate the mob.

8 **James Joseph 'Whitey' Bulger, Jr** – Crime kingpin in South Boston, Massachusetts. Played by Jack Nicholson in *The Departed*, his name changed to Francis 'Frank' Costello. In the film, Costello dies in a shoot-out with police following a drug bust. In reality, Bulger is still alive and serving life for his crimes.

9 **Mickey Cohen** – Ruthless Los Angeles crime boss of the 1940s and 1950s, played by Sean Penn in *Gangster Squad*. In the film, Cohen was jailed for murder and ended up in Alcatraz. In real life, he was jailed for tax evasion in 1961 but, having survived a murder attempt, was freed in 1972. Diagnosed with stomach cancer, Cohen died in his sleep in 1976, aged 62.

10 **James Burke** – A New York Lucchese crime family associate. Portrayed by Robert De Niro in *Goodfellas*, his name changed to Jimmy 'The Gent' Conway. In the film, Conway is last seen serving a 20-year-to-life sentence in a New York State prison. In reality, he died in prison in 1996, the cause of death lung cancer, aged 64.

Top 10 sexiest female film characters of all time*

CHARACTER	FILM/YEAR	ACTOR
1 **Brigitte Latour**	*Naughty Girl* (1956)	Brigitte Bardot
2 **Lara Croft**	*Lara Croft Tomb Raider: The Cradle of Life* (2003)	Angelina Jolie
3 **Vesper Lynd**	*Casino Royale* (2006)	Eva Green
4 **Leeloo**	*The Fifth Element* (1997)	Milla Jovovich
5 **Sugar Kane**	*Some Like It Hot* (1959)	Marilyn Monroe
6 **Holly Golightly**	*Breakfast at Tiffany's* (1961)	Audrey Hepburn
7 **Natacha Von Braun**	*Alphaville* (1965)	Anna Karina
8 **Princess Leia**	*Star Wars: Episodes IV–VI* (1977–83)	Carrie Fisher
9 **Selene**	*Underworld* series (2003, 2006, 2009 and 2012)	Kate Beckinsale
10 **Mia Wallace**	*Pulp Fiction* (1994)	Uma Thurman

*According to Death By Films, November 2013
Source: Death By Films, www.deathbyfilms.com

10 other (lesser known) rules of *Fight Club*

1 No pinching. Don't be that guy.

2 If you see Tyler talking to himself, just let that go. He's cool.

3 No capes. Why do we even have to address this?

4 No drawing on a guy's face if he's knocked out unless it's really, really funny.

5 Tag team matches are only allowed if you wear matching face paint.

6 Stop flushing paper towels down the toilet. It's doing a real number on the plumbing.

7 If one of Bob's breasts falls out during a fight let him put it away. We don't want to see that again.

8 Put your phone on silent. Seriously guys, it's rude.

9 If you must talk about *Fight Club*, please don't do it in a Borat voice, OK?

10 If you make a flyer, use a good font. No one takes us seriously in Comic Sans.

Source: Mandatory.com; see www.mandatory.com for more

10 memorable film robots

1 **T-1000** (*Terminator 2: Judgment Day*, 1991) – More menacingly memorable than Arnie's Cyberdyne Systems Model 101 in the original, the shape-shifting next-generation Terminator is sent back to finish the job Schwarzenegger failed to complete – kill John Connor. Impervious to pain and seemingly unstoppable.

2 **H.A.L. 9000** (*2001: A Space Odyssey*, 1968) – Primary antagonist of *Space Odyssey*, the Heuristically programmed ALgorithmic computer controls the systems of the *Discovery One* spacecraft. And, despite being little more than a small red eye, he became perhaps the most influential robot in the history of film.

3 **R2-D2** (*Star Wars*, 1977) – Made even more admirable by simply not being the doddering old dear C-3PO, the little rolling robot was equipped to deal with any situation – extinguishing fires, projecting vital holograms and providing emergency repairs to spacecraft. Quietly and efficiently heroic.

4 **RoboCop** (*RoboCop*, 1987) – In a hellish vision of the future, crime-ravaged Detroit is policed by a single hybrid law enforcement office – part man, part machine, all bionic patrolman. Answers to the name Murphy, brought back from the dead to serve, protect and exact swift, efficient and admirable justice.

5 **WALL-E** (*WALL-E*, 2008) – In a far-distant future, a small, waste-collecting robot (Waste Allocation Load Lifter, Earth Class) inadvertently embarks on a space journey that decides the fate of humanity, and falls in love. An oddly moving critique of the path trodden by the human race.

6 **Agent Smith** (*The Matrix*, 1999) – Primary antagonist of *The Matrix* trilogy, de facto leader of 'The Agents', a program created by the Matrix to rid the system of any disruptive resistance. Initially deleted, Smith evolves into a virus, which threatens to overwhelm everything.

7 **Optimus Prime** (*Transformers*, 1986) – Alien leader of the heroic Autobots, a faction of transforming robots from the planet Cybertron, present on Earth to prevent the rival, transforming Decepticons discovering the All Spark. Brave, wise, just and hard as nails.

8 **Fembots** (*Austin Powers*, 1997) – For the latest word in android replicant technology – bring out the Fembots, a collection of buxom blonde beauties armed with machine gun breasts. Defeated by Powers but sent back in subsequent sequels, most memorably in the form of Britney Spears. If Hugh Hefner made robots...

9 **Evil Bill and Ted** (*Bill and Ted's Bogus Journey*, 1991) – Evil robot doppelgängers of the titular heroes, created by the scheming Chuck De Nomolos to prevent the real Bill and Ted from winning the San Dimas Battle of the Bands by killing them. Pretty heinous, but ultimately excellent.

10 **SICO** (*Rocky IV*, 1985) – Appearing from out of nowhere and for no clear or rational reason, SICO was the weird robot servant Rocky bought Paulie for his birthday. Back in 1985, it no doubt seemed inevitable that every house would soon be served by one. Almost three decades on, we're still waiting.

10 great porn film parodies

1. *Tits a Wonderful Life*

2. *Riding Miss Daisy*

3. *White Men Can't Hump*

4. *Whorrey Potter & the Sorcerer's Balls*

5. *Good Will Humping*

6. *Shaving Ryan's Privates*

7. *Schindler's Fist*

8. *Forrest Hump*

9. *Raiders of the Lost Arse*

10. *Jurassic Pork*

10 finest porn star names

PORN NAME	REAL NAME
1 Lexington Steele	Clifton Todd Britt Jr
2 Randy Spears	Gregory Allan Deuschle
3 Michael J. Cox	Troy Edward Ballou
4 Dale DaBone	Dale Newton Rutter
5 Ben Dover	Simon Honey
6 Jack Hammer	Troy Mainwaring
7 Arnold Schwarzenpecker	Schmuel Berkowitz
8 Danny Mountain	Danny Mountain*
9 Wilde Oscar	Christopher Norman
10 Long Dong Silver	Daniel Arthur Mead

*A former Southampton FC footballer

FILM

Top 10 superheroes*

SUPERHERO	VIDEO CLIPS (HOURS)	YOUTUBE VIEWS†
❶ Batman	71,000	3 billion
❷ Thor	66,000	2 billion
❸ Superman	14,000	1.7 billion
❹ Iron Man	20,000	1.4 billion
❺ The Avengers	31,000	1 billion
❻ Wolverine	7,800	540 million
❼ Spider Man	7,400	340 million
❽ Captain America	4,900	280 million
❾ Justice League	3,200	220 million
❿ Deadpool	8,900	200 million

*Ranked by YouTube views

†Total number of views of 'film trailers, video game play, fan originals and more' for all superheroes on YouTube as at 7 August 2013

Source: 'YouTube Trends', http://youtube-trends.blogspot.co.uk

You might also find it interesting to note that while Batman takes the top overall spot for views, the Dark Knight has been overtaken in the search category by Thor, Iron Man and The Avengers since 2008.

Top 10 toughest superheroes (in the DC Universe)*

FILM

SUPERHERO	INTELLIGENCE	STRENGTH	SPEED	AGILITY	FIGHTING	TOTAL POINTS
1 Superman	7	50	19	21	87	184
2 Martian Manhunter	6	46	18	21	85	176
3 Supergirl	3	45	17	18	85	168
4 Wonder Woman	7	41	18	19	78	163
5 Batman	8	31	7	17	92	155
5 The Flash	4	27	20	25	79	155
7 Batgirl	4	29	7	19	90	149
7 Bane	6	38	6	14	85	149
9 Nightwing	7	26	6	17	80	136
9 Hawkman	4	30	8	17	77	136
Notable others:						
Green Lantern	*4*	*26*	*12*	*13*	*80*	*135*
Robin	*6*	*24*	*5*	*16*	*67*	*118*
The Joker	*7*	*22*	*4*	*12*	*70*	*115*
The Riddler	*5*	*18*	*4*	*13*	*64*	*104*
Ra's Al Ghul	*7*	*24*	*4*	*14*	*80*	*129*
The Penguin	*7*	*18*	*3*	*8*	*62*	*98*

*Based on *Top Trumps DC Universe Heroes and Villains* rankings

Source: Top Trumps, www.toptrumps.com

10 of Batman's less fearsome enemies

1 **The Eraser** – A boyhood buddy of Bruce Wayne, the Eraser was the marvellously monikered Lenny Fiasco, who turned to crime as a villain who erased the evidence of other criminals' crimes for a cut of the profit. He wouldn't have been so lame had he not dressed as a pencil, with a rubber for a head.

2 **Kite Man** – Blessed with a piece of canvas strapped to his back, this allowed him to fly through the air at a very average rate of knots. He flew quicker when dropped off Wayne Tower by Deathstroke, without the kite, a drop that almost killed him.

3 **Calendar Man** – A low-grade villain so obsessed by calendars, they eventually turned him mad. Calendar Man commits his crimes on key dates, making him one of history's most predictable villains. And he dresses like a calendar, making him highly conspicuous, even down a darkened street.

4 **The Condiment King** – Armed with bottles of mustard and ketchup for weapons, and a big bag of lame, condiment-based puns ('How I relished this meeting', 'I knew you'd ketchup with me', and so forth), this villainous clown was being brainwashed by the Joker. Clearly, he didn't, ahem, cut the mustard.

5 **The Ventriloquist and Scarface** – Arnold Wesker was a tedious ventriloquist with a wooden gangster puppet on the end of his arm and an annoying inability to pronounce his words correctly – for years referring to 'Gatman'. The dummy called all the shots, until finally, he was shot into a million splinters.

Firefly – Real name Garfield Lynns, a super-villain with no discernible superpowers. An arsonist by trade, but inept enough to blow up a chemical plant and suffer heinous burns in the process.

Killer Moth – Adopting the identity of millionaire philanthropist Cameron van Cleer, Killer Moth was revealed to be Drury Walker, a hopeless hoodlum with the truly terrifying abilities of a moth. He found himself beaten up by Batgirl, unsurprisingly.

Ten-eyed Man – In theory, Philip Reardon's alter ego had potential – a blind Vietnam vet who had his optic nerves reattached to his fingertips. His vision was first-rate; only Batman had his measure, defeating him more than once by tempting the gullible sod into catching painful objects.

Humpty Dumpty – Real name Humphry Dumpler, a hulking numbskull of a man with a mechanical mind and a compulsion to take stuff apart so he can put it back together again. More tedious than in any way terrifying.

Crazy Quilt – Painter and master thief, his 'real' identity unknown. Capable of seeing only the most intense colours, Crazy Quilt ignored the basics of criminal evasion by dressing in a crazy quilt, fashioned into a crazy suit, topped off with a crazy mind-controlling helmet. Crazy name, crap villain.

Top 10 *Star Wars* villains*

CHARACTER/S	DARK SIDE POINTS
1 **Emperor Palpatine** (Empire)†	25
2 **Darth Maul** (Sith Lord)	24
3 **Darth Vader** (Darth Vader)	23
4 **Count Dooku** (Separatist)	21
=5 **Jabba the Hutt** (Criminal)	20
=5 **Boba Fett** (Bounty Hunter)	20
=5 **Commander Cody** (Republic)	20
=5 **General Grievous** (Separatist)	20
=5 **Jango Fett** (Bounty Hunter)	20
=10 **Imperial Stormtroopers** (Empire)	19
=10 **Droideka** (Droid)	19
=10 **Grievous' Bodyguard** (Separatist)	19
=10 **Admiral Ozzel** (Mr Bronson from *Grange Hill*)	19

*Based on characters featuring in *Top Trumps Star Wars edition, Episodes I–VI* and ranked by 'Dark Side' points

†As Chancellor Palpatine (Republic) 22 Dark Side points.

Source: Top Trumps, www.toptrumps.com

For reference and some kind of contrast, note the Dark Side statistics of the galaxy's good guys. Yoda, R2-D2 and C-3PO all register 0. Obi-Wan Kenobi and Princess Leia Organa are both 1. Luke Skywalker is a 4. And the opportunist smuggler Han Solo a 6. The conflicted Jedi Anakin Skywalker ranks an 18, for he is obviously 'on the turn'.

10 fictional characters on Hollywood's Walk of Fame

CHARACTER/S	YEAR INDUCTED	ADDRESS
1 **Mickey Mouse***	1978	6925 Hollywood Boulevard
2 **Bugs Bunny**	1985	7007 Hollywood Boulevard
3 **Woody Woodpecker**	1990	7000 Hollywood Boulevard
4 **Big Bird**	1994	7021 Hollywood Boulevard
5 **The Simpsons**	2000	7021 Hollywood Boulevard
6 **Kermit the Frog**	2002	6801 Hollywood Boulevard
7 **Godzilla**	2004	6925 Hollywood Boulevard
8 **Donald Duck**	2004	6840 Hollywood Boulevard
9 **Shrek**	2010	6931 Hollywood Boulevard
10 **The Muppets**	2012	6834 Hollywood Boulevard

*First animated character inducted

The Hollywood Walk of Fame honours notable figures in the film, television, music, radio and theatre industries. Each figure has been awarded a Walk of Fame star, which can be located up and down both sides of Hollywood Boulevard.

Top 10 ways soap characters die

MANNER OF DEATH	TOTAL DEATHS
1 Murder	66
2 Heart attack	60
3 Car accident	54
4 Cancer	26
5 Suicide	25
6 A fall	16
=7 Shot	11
=7 Stroke	11
9 Run over	10
10 Drowning	8

*In *Coronation Street*, *EastEnders*, *Home & Away*, *Neighbours*, *Emmerdale (Farm)*, *Hollyoaks* and *The Archers* between 1 January 1951 and 1 January 2011

Source: Figures collated by *Delayed Gratification* magazine, www.dgquarterly.com

0 unusual soap character deaths*

1. Abseiling accident

2. Asbestos poisoning

3. Barn fire

4. Bull attack

5. Bush fire

6. Euthanasia pact

7. Gangrene

8. Mudslide

9. Shark attack

10. Tram crash

*In *Coronation Street*, *EastEnders*, *Home & Away*, *Neighbours*, *Emmerdale (Farm)*, *Hollyoaks* and *The Archers* between 1 January 1951 and 1 January 2011

Source: *Delayed Gratification* magazine, www.dgquarterly.com

Each of the above was responsible for a single death.

Top 10 greatest US TV series*

TELEVISION

SERIES	CREATED BY	AIRED
1 *The Sopranos*	David Chase	1999–200?
2 *Seinfeld*	Larry David and Jerry Seinfeld	1989–98
3 *The Twilight Zone*	Rod Serling	1959–64
4 *All in the Family*	Johnny Speight	1971–9
5 *M*A*S*H*	Larry Gelbart†	1972–83
6 *The Mary Tyler Moore Show*	James L. Brooks and Allan Burns	1970–77
7 *Mad Men*	Matthew Weiner	2007–present
8 *Cheers*	Glen Charles, Les Charles and James Burrows	1982–93
9 *The Wire*	David Simon	2002–8
10 *The West Wing*	Aaron Sorkin	1999–2006

*Based on the Best Written TV Series as voted for by The Writers Guild of America, taken from a 101-strong list

†Developed *M*A*S*H* for television

Source: 101 Best Written TV Series, www.wga.org

Top 10 British TV ads*

1 **Hovis: 'Bike'** (1973) – Flat-cap delivery boy struggles uphill with a loaf of bread.

2 **Smash: 'Martians'** (1974) – Tin aliens laugh at reports that humans eat real potatoes.

3 **John Smith's Bitter: 'Dog'** (1983) – Magical dog, performs tricks for a bowl of bitter.

4 **British Gas: 'Tell Sid'** (1986) – Small, idyllic-looking town spreads word of British Gas shares. Sid never finds out.

5 **Milk: 'Accrington Stanley'** (1988) – Footballers who don't drink milk will only ever play for Accrington Stanley, claim kids, back when they advertised milk.

6 **British Airways: 'Face'** (1989) – Bringing people together, literally, as two eyes, a mouth, a nose and some ears combine to form a face in the desert.

7 **Carling: 'Dambusters'** (1989) – Brave lone soldier assumes goalkeeper role and saves series of bouncing bombs. 'I bet he drinks Carling Black Label,' marvel pilots.

8 **Reebok: 'Theatre Of Dreams'** (1998) – Assorted celebrities, among them Tom Jones, Robbie Williams and George Best, narrate the build-up to a Ryan Giggs goal; Jimmy Hill is bound and gagged.

9 **Sony: 'Bravia Balls'** (2005) – Multicoloured balls bounce down hills of San Francisco, selling colour televisions and causing a mess.

10 **Halfords: 'The Trip'** (2012) – Family embarks on 1970s camping trip, gets rained on, grows up, goes camping again. 'The best trips last a lifetime.'

*Based on a marketing and media company poll of creative directors at advertising and marketing agencies, who were asked to name their most memorable British advert ever to mark the Queen's Diamond Jubilee, 2012

Source: The Drum, www.thedrum.com

Top 10 greatest albums of all time*

ALBUM/YEAR	GROUP
① *OK Computer* (1997) Appears in 850 charts Rank score†: 112,447	Radiohead
② *The Dark Side of the Moon* (1973) Appears in 1,690 charts Rank score: 99,616	Pink Floyd
③ *Revolver* (1966) Appears in 1,540 charts Rank score: 90,374	The Beatles
④ *Abbey Road* (1969) Appears in 1,467 charts Rank score: 86,214	The Beatles
⑤ *Sgt. Pepper's Lonely Hearts Club Band* (1967) Appears in 1,464 charts Rank score: 82,621	The Beatles
⑥ *Nevermind* (1991) Appears in 1,356 charts Rank score: 66,736	Nirvana
⑦ *Led Zeppelin IV* (1971) Appears in 1,267 charts Rank score: 62,858	Led Zeppelin

ALBUM/YEAR	GROUP

The Beatles (The White Album) (1968) — The Beatles
Appears in 1,200 charts
Rank score: 62,279

Funeral (2004) — Arcade Fire
Appears in 1,217 charts
Rank score: 61,893

Kid A (2000) — Radiohead
Appears in 1,241 charts
Rank score: 61,565

*Based on an album's position in more than 12,000 greatest album charts posted by users on BestEverAlbums.com. The higher the position in individual charts, the greater the points awarded (the 'rank score')

†As at December 2013

Source: www.BestEverAlbums.com

Top 10 singles of all time*

MUSIC

SONG	ARTIST/GROUP	ALBUM/YEAR
❶ 'A Day in the Life'	The Beatles	*Sgt. Pepper's Lonely Hearts Club Band* (1967)
❷ 'Like a Rolling Stone'	Bob Dylan	*Highway 61 Revisited* (1965)
❸ 'Paranoid Android'	Radiohead	*OK Computer* (1997)
❹ 'Time'	Pink Floyd	*The Dark Side of the Moon* (1973)
❺ 'Bohemian Rhapsody'	Queen	*A Night at the Opera* (1975)
❻ 'Wish You Were Here'	Pink Floyd	*Wish You Were Here* (1975)
❼ 'Stairway to Heaven'	Led Zeppelin	*Led Zeppelin IV* (1971)
❽ 'Comfortably Numb'	Pink Floyd	*The Wall* (1979)
❾ 'Shine On You Crazy Diamond, Parts I-V'	Pink Floyd	*Wish You Were Here* (1975)
❿ 'While My Guitar Gently Weeps'	The Beatles	*The Beatles (The White Album)* (1968)

*According to Best Ever Albums, a website that ranks albums and singles based on user votes to provide an aggregate score. The tracks here received the highest average rating, graded out of 100. Ranking correct as at December 2013

Source: Best Ever Albums, www.BestEverAlbums.com

The 10 worst albums of the last 25 years*

ALBUM/YEAR	ARTIST/GROUP	GENRE
1 *Crazy Frog Presents Crazy Hits* (2005)	Crazy Frog	Novelty, Dance-Pop, Electronic
2 *I'm Not a Fan, But the Kids Like It!* (2009)	BrokeNCYDE	Crunkcore, Crunk, Electropop
3 *Souljaboytellem.com* (2007)	Soulja Boy Tell 'Em	Snap, Pop Rap
4 *The Unspoken King* (2008)	Cryptopsy	Deathcore
5 *Illud Divinum Insanus* (2011)	Morbid Angel	Death Metal
6 *St. Anger* (2003)	Metallica	Alternative Metal
7 *My World 2.0* (2010)	Justin Bieber	Teen Pop
8 *Lulu* (2011)	Lou Reed and Metallica	Heavy Metal
9 *Masturbate in Praise of Black Satan* (1992)	Apator	A Cappella, Spoken Word
10 *The E.N.D.* (2009)	The Black Eyed Peas	Pop Rap, Electropop

*As ranked by the users of www.rateyourmusic.com. RYM is a global community-built music database where users rate music. Ranking covers UK users only and is correct as at December 2013

Source: www.rateyourmusic.com

10 memorable country music song titles

MUSIC

1 **'Get Your Biscuits in the Oven, and Your Buns in the Bed'**
– Kinky Friedman

2 **'She Thinks My Tractor's Sexy'** – Kenny Chesney

3 **'I Went Back to My Fourth Wife for the Third Time and Gave Her a Second Chance to Make a First Class Fool Out of Me'**
– Rev. Billy C. Wirtz

4 **'How Can I Miss You If You Won't Go Away?'** – Leonard Linnehan and Louis Philip Perry

5 **'Tequila Makes Her Clothes Fall Off'** – Joe Nichols

6 **'Her Teeth Were Stained, But Her Heart Was Pure'** – Robin Dorsey

7 **'Are You Drinkin' With Me Jesus?'** – Jello Biafra & Mojo Nixon

8 **'You're the Reason Our Kids Are So Ugly'** – Loretta Lynn

9 **'Get Off the Table, Mabel (The Two Dollars Is for the Beer)'**
– Bull Moose Jackson and the Flashcats

10 **'Get Your Tongue Outta My Mouth 'Cause I'm Kissing You Goodbye'** – Ray Stevens

10 famous bands who changed their names

1 **Red Hot Chili Peppers** were **Tony Flow and the Miraculously Majestic Masters of Mayhem** – Tony being lead singer Anthony Kiedis. The original name lasted until 1983.

2 **Radiohead** were **On a Friday** – At school they rehearsed on a Frid… Yeah, you get it. Inspired to change their name by the Talking Heads track 'Radio Head'.

3 **R.E.M.** were **Can of Piss** – Just one of several possible names the band reportedly toyed with, alongside Twisted Kites and the charming Slut Bank.

4 **Barenaked Ladies** were **Free Beer** – Both of which were just false promises to gullible gig goers.

5 **Jimi Hendrix Experience** were **Jimmy James & the Blue Flames** – Replaced within a few months with a grand promise and an alternative spelling of the Seattle star's name.

6 **Pearl Jam** were **Mookie Blaylock** – Originally named after the NBA point guard, until it became a legal issue. The new name was reportedly a nod to Eddie Vedder's great grandmother who made a peyote jam, though Vedder claims this is not true.

7 **U2** were **The Hype** – Bono and his bandmates were supposedly offered six options from which to choose a new name. U2 was apparently the one they disliked the least.

8 **Pink Floyd** were **The Screaming Abdabs** – Before taking their new name, based on two legendary Blues musicians (Pink Anderson and Floyd Council), the band toyed with Tea Set, the Meggadeaths and Sigma 6.

9 **Van Halen** were **Rat Salad** – Previously known as Mammoth, Van Halen briefly also contemplated Rat Salad (after the Black Sabbath track rather than serving suggestion), but not for long.

10 **Led Zeppelin** were **The New Yardbirds** – When legal issues forced a rename, Led Zeppelin was born, the name reportedly originating from a joke that the band would go down like a lead balloon, and 'Lead' becoming 'Led' so as not to confuse less educated US fans.

10 musicians who once had 'proper' jobs

1 **Sting** – Was once a teacher at a convent school, teaching English, music and football.

2 **Mick Jagger** – While attending London School of Economics, Jagger worked as a porter at a psychiatric hospital.

3 **Ozzy Osbourne** – Previously worked as a construction worker, a trainee plumber, in a morgue and in a slaughterhouse.

4 **Kurt Cobain** – Made ends meet working as a janitor, sweeping floor and cleaning toilets.

5 **Jack White** – The male half of the White Stripes ran his own upholstery business before fame came a calling.

6 **Diddy** – Before becoming Puff Daddy and then Diddy, plain old Sean John Combs cleaned the toilets in a gas station.

7 **Rod Stewart** – Not so many people thought Rod Stewart was sexy when he was a grave digger at Highgate Cemetery.

8 **Madonna** – In the early '80s, 'Madge' worked at a Dunkin' Donuts in Times Square, New York.

9 **Johnny Cash** – The future 'Man in Black' was previously a man in the US Army, where he worked as a Military Code Breaker.

10 **Chris Cornell** – The frontman of Soundgarden worked as a seafood wholesaler before grunge came a calling.

10 untimely rock star deaths

1 **Elvis Presley** – Legend has it that 'The King' died on, or at least near, the toilet, the cause of death most likely heart complications caused by prescription drug addiction. It was 1977 and he was 42.

2 **John Bonham** – The legendary Led Zeppelin drummer overdosed on vodka in 1980, aged 32. A verdict of accidental death was returned, caused by Bonham downing around 40 shots of vodka and choking on his own vomit.

3 **Jerry Garcia** – The heavily bearded Grateful Dead frontman died in August 1995 following a heart attack thought to have been brought on by drug addiction. He was 53.

4 **Michael Hutchence** – Theories split between his death being a tragic episode of accidental autoerotic asphyxiation or that the INXS frontman chose suicide in his hotel room. He left the stage in 1997, aged 37.

5 **Tim Buckley** – Jeff's dad overdosed on heroin in 1975, allegedly thinking it was cocaine but most likely the result of mixing drugs with an excessive quantity of alcohol. He was 28.

6 **Jeff Buckley** – Tim's son overdosed on misadventure in 1997, drowning in the Mississippi. There were no signs of drink, drugs or suicide and his death was not considered mysterious. He was 30.

7 **2Pac and Biggie** – They come as one, both shot dead in a rap 'beef'. 2Pac met his end in Las Vegas in 1996, aged 25; Biggie (aka the Notorious B.I.G.) in a possible act of retaliation in New York in 1997, aged 24.

8 **Marvin Gaye** – Shot dead by his father, Marvin Gaye Snr, in 1984, aged 44, following an argument over a business issue. The gun used had been a gift given by Gaye to his father the previous Christmas.

9 **Keith Moon –** Too much drink and too many drugs finally took their toll on the wild man of rock, though his death in 1978 was attributed to an overdose of a drug designed to curb alcohol abuse. He was 31.

10 **Sid Vicious** – Died of a heroin overdose in 1979, reportedly administered by his own mother. Vicious was 21.

10 tragic members of 'The 27 Club'*

1 Alexandre Levy – The first of the gang to die, Levy was a Brazilian composer, pianist and conductor who died in January 1892. His cause of death remains unconfirmed.

2 Rudy Lewis – Best known for his work with the Drifters, singer Lewis was found dead in a Harlem hotel room in May 1964, most likely taken by a heinous combination of drugs, asphyxiation and a heart attack.

3 Brian Jones – Founder member of the Rolling Stones, Jones battled drink, drugs and depression and died by 'misadventure': he drowned in his swimming pool in 1969.

4 Janis Joplin – Charismatic but troubled American singer, Joplin overdosed six times in 1969 alone and finally died alone in a Los Angeles hotel room the following year, overdosing on heroin.

5 Jimi Hendrix – Mixing wine with a large quantity of sleeping pills and then going to bed proved fatal for the guitar legend in 1970. The 'Voodoo Child' choked to death on his own vomit.

6 Jim Morrison – The troubled frontman of Los Angeles four-piece, the Doors, and a frequent fan of alcohol and drugs, Morrison was found dead in the bath of his Paris apartment in 1971, having overdosed on heroin.

7 **Ron McKernan** – Founding member of Grateful Dead, 'Pigpen' was found dead at his home in California in March 1973, having succumbed to Crohn's disease. The illness also claimed the life of his brother.

8 **Kurt Cobain** – In 1994, with his band Nirvana having broken through to music's mainstream, Cobain wrote a suicide note, injected heroin and shot himself. 'Now he's gone and joined that stupid club,' his mother said. 'I told him not to.'

9 **Richey Edwards** – Troubled Manic Street Preacher, Edwards has not been seen since early 1995 and was declared 'presumed dead' in November 2008. At the time of his disappearance he was aged 27.

10 **Amy Winehouse** – Multi-award-winning soul singer who struggled with drink and drug dependency and was found dead at her Camden home in July 2011. Tests confirmed she died of accidental alcohol poisoning.

*Famous musicians who died aged 27

10 unexpected duets

1 **Eminem and Elton John** ('Stan', 2001) – Unexpected in that one was a gay icon while the other was a rapper with a number of homophobic lyrics to his name. At the 2001 Grammys, the pair teamed up and an unlikely friendship was born.

2 **Freddie Mercury and Montserrat Caballé** ('Barcelona', 1987) – Reflecting the flamboyant Queen frontman's love of opera, evident in the likes of 'Bohemian Rhapsody', this warbling mash-up with the Spanish operatic soprano led to a full-blown album of the same name.

3 **Paul McCartney and some frogs (the 'Frog Chorus')** ('We All Stand Together', 1984) – On the back of an animated film, McCartney teamed up with some singing frogs on a single that bothered the top of the charts in 1984. Evidently spent of creativity, the B-side was a stripped-back, humming version of the same song.

4 **Nick Cave and Kylie Minogue** ('Where the Wild Roses Grow', 1995) – The dark prince of murder ballads takes clean-cut Kylie down to the river and kills her with a rock. And none of us expected that.

5 **Paul McCartney and Stevie Wonder** ('Ebony and Ivory', 1982) – Pre-Frog Chorus, Macca gave the double thumbs up to a duet with Stevie Wonder on a track about the black and white keys on a piano. Actually, thinking about it now, there may have been a deeper meaning to it.

6 **Willie Nelson and Snoop Dogg** ('Superman', 2011) – Willie Nelson featuring Snoop Dogg, or Snoop Dogg featuring Willie Nelson? Unlikely either way, though a shared love of 'herbal' fags made this less unexpected than we might have otherwise thought.

7 Tony Bennett and Lady Gaga ('The Lady Is A Tramp', 2011) – The curious coming together of celebrated octogenarian crooner and the shape-shifting, agent provocateur to be found on his album *Duets II*. The lady is a tramp? Not Gaga, certainly. According to Bennett, she's a real 'jazz lady'.

8 James Brown and Luciano Pavarotti ('It's a Man's World', 2002) – The oddest of the duets Pavarotti pulled together for his annual Pavarotti & Friends concert, with the corpulent tenor going head to head with the thrusting Godfather of Soul himself.

9 Texas and Method Man ('Say What You Want', 1998) – On paper, the Wu-Tang clan reworking of a middle-of-the-road Texas track shouldn't have worked. In reality, it didn't. Meth's rap jarred painfully with Sharleen Spiteri's comical attempts to 'keep it real' by breathing heavily and walking like a ho'. Not to be repeated.

10 Bing Crosby and David Bowie ('The Little Drummer Boy/Peace on Earth', 1977) – In which the Thin White Duke nipped round to the castle of his neighbour – Sir Percival – and, following a passage of stilted Christmas-themed conversation, tinkled the ivories with the butler, the boy Crosby. By some distance the most surreal encounter on this list.

10 songs with bizarre hidden messages*

1. **'Several Species of Small Furry Animals Gathered Together in a Cave and Grooving With a Pict'** (Pink Floyd) – At around 4:32, if played at half speed and you listen really hard, 'That was pretty avant-garde, wasn't it?' can be heard.

2. **'Work It'** (Missy Elliot) – Just after two minutes in, the listener is instructed: 'Listen up close while I take you backwards', after which the lyrics played backwards are, 'Watch the way Missy like to take it backwards.'

3. **'Another One Bites the Dust'** (Queen) – Denied by their management and passed off as phonetic reversal, Queen's 1980 track allegedly contains the phrase 'It's fun to smoke marijuana'.

4. **'Stairway to Heaven'** (Led Zeppelin) – In the middle section, during the 'If there's a bustle in your hedgerow, don't be alarmed now' passage, the phrase 'Here's to my sweet Satan' can supposedly be heard.

5. **'Revolution 9'** (The Beatles) – The song is alleged to contain the instruction: 'Turn me on, dead man', giving weight to the conspiracy theory that Paul McCartney has been dead since 1966 (see page 270).

6. **'Revelation #9'** (Marilyn Manson) – A man with a supposed penchant for backmasking. In this song, 'If anyone's playing this backwards. How you doing? How you doing?' can be heard, before he begins to make lewd remarks about your mother.

7 **'Empty Spaces'** (Pink Floyd) – One of the clearer instances, the track from *The Wall* contains the message: 'Congratulations. You have just discovered the secret message. Please send your answer to Old Pink, care of the Funny Farm.'

8 **'Detour Thru Your Mind'** (The B-52s) – Contains the line: 'I buried my parakeet in the backyard. Oh no, you're playing the record backwards. Watch out, you might ruin your needle.'

9 **'Better By You, Better By Me'** (Judas Priest) – One of the most infamous accusations of backmasking came in 1985 when two men attempted suicide after supposedly hearing the instruction: 'Do it!' A lawsuit was issued, and later dismissed.

10 **'Fire On High'** (ELO) – The song on which the hairy Brummies supposedly slipped in the warning: 'The music is reversible, but time is not. Turn back! Turn back! Turn back! Turn back!'

*When the songs are played backwards, often termed 'backmasking'

Some claim the hidden and sometimes subliminal messages in the songs are clear, others that it is simply a case of phonetic reversal; and some are far more audible than others.

Top 10 misquoted song lyrics of all time*

MISQUOTED LYRIC/SONG/ARTIST/CORRECT LYRIC	PERCENTAGE†

1 **'Sweet dreams are made of cheese'** ('Sweet Dreams', Eurythmics). Correct lyric is: 'Sweet dreams are made of this'. — 28%

2 **'We found dove in a soapless place'** ('We Found Love', Rihanna). Correct lyric is: 'We found love in a hopeless place'. — 26%

3 **'Can't stand gravy'** ('Constant Craving', k.d. lang) Correct lyric is: 'Constant craving'. — 20%

4 **'Do it like a lady'** ('Dude Looks Like a Lady', Aerosmith) Correct lyric is: 'Dude looks like a lady'. — 10%

5 **'Peggy, Peggy Suuuuue'** ('Beggin', Madcon) Correct lyric is: 'Beggin, beggin youuuu'. — 7%

=6 **'Every time you go away, you take a piece of meat with you'** ('Every Time You Go Away', Paul Young) Correct lyric is: 'Every time you go away, you take a piece of me with you'. — 3%

=6 **'Hold me close now Tony Danza'** ('Tiny Dancer', Elton John) Correct lyric is: 'Hold me closer tiny dancer'. — 3%

=8 **'Daddy I've fallen for a lobster'** ('Black Heart', Stooshe) Correct lyric is: 'Daddy I've fallen for a monster'. — 1%

=8 **'Hey ho, gotta let go'** ('Dynamite', Taio Cruz) Correct lyric is: 'Hey ho galileo'. — 1%

=8 **'It doesn't make a difference if we're naked or not'** ('Living on a Prayer', Bon Jovi) Correct lyric is: 'It doesn't make a difference if we make it or not'. — 1%

*According to digital music service Spotify, who polled 1,379 music fans to establish the songs most often misquoted

†List correct as at June 2013

Source: www.spotify.com

10 singers who reached UK Number 1 despite being dead

ARTIST	SONG

1 Buddy Holly — 'It Doesn't Matter Anymore'
Died February 1959 in a plane crash; reached Number 1 in April 1959.

2 Jimi Hendrix — 'Voodoo Chile'
Died September 1970 from a drugs overdose; reached Number 1 in November 1970.

3 John Lennon* — '(Just Like) Starting Over'
Was shot, and died on 8 December 1980; reached Number 1 two weeks later.

4 Jackie Wilson — 'Reet Petite (The Sweetest Girl in Town)' (reissue)
Died January 1984 from pneumonia; reached Number 1 in November 1986.

5 Freddie Mercury† — 'Living On My Own'
Died November 1991 from bronchial pneumonia resulting from AIDS; reached Number 1 in August 1993.

6 Aaliyah — 'More Than a Woman'
Died August 2001 in a plane crash; reached Number 1 in January 2002.

7 George Harrison — 'My Sweet Lord' (reissue)
Died November 2001 from cancer; reached Number 1 in January 2002.

8 2Pac — 'Ghetto Gospel' (featuring Elton John)
Was shot, and died September 1996; reached Number 1 in July 2005.

9 The Notorious B.I.G. — 'Nasty Girl' (with Diddy, Nelly, Jagged Edge and Avery Storm)
Was shot, and died March 1997; reached Number 1 in February 2006.

10 Eva Cassidy — 'What a Wonderful World' (with Katie Melua)
Died November 1996 from cancer; reached Number 1 in December 2007.

*Also reached Number 1 with the release of 'Imagine' (a re-entry) in January 1981 and 'Woman' in February 1981

†Also reached Number 1 with Queen following the reissue of 'Bohemian Rhapsody/These Are The Days Of Our Lives' in December 1991

10 songs 'banned' by the BBC

1 **'With My Little Stick of Blackpool Rock'** (George Formby, 1937) – The problem, ruled Auntie when banning this one, was that while Formby said 'stick of rock', the master of the mischievous double entendre meant something significantly different.

2 **'Lucy in the Sky with Diamonds'** (The Beatles, 1967) – Banned for its supposed drug references, though the Beatles denied any intent.

3 **'Let's Spend the Night Together'** (The Rolling Stones, 1967) – Banned for supposedly promoting promiscuity, which Auntie deemed unacceptable even in the swinging sixties.

4 **'Lola'** (The Kinks , 1970) – It contravened the corporation's no advertising rules, courtesy of the line 'You drink champagne and it tastes just like Coca-Cola' – quickly rerecorded as 'cherry cola' to avert the ban.

5 **'Love to Love You Baby'** (Donna Summer, 1976) – Banned because it contained some frisky sex noises.

6 **'God Save the Queen'** (The Sex Pistols, 1977) – Considered 'gross bad taste', in part due to the refrain 'God save the queen, the fascist regime'.

7 **'I Want Your Sex'** (George Michael, 1987) – Banned pre-watershed, for the supposedly subversive subject and suggestion: 'Sex is natural/Sex is good/Not everybody does it/But everybody should!'

8 **'We Call it Acieed'** (D-Mob, 1988) – Glorified the consumption of class-A drugs, in this case the acid in the burgeoning Acid House scene.

9 **'Ebeneezer Goode'** (The Shamen, 1992) – The refrain 'Eezer Goode, 'Eezer Goode/He's Ebeneezer Goode' was fooling no one.

10 **'Smack My Bitch Up'** (The Prodigy, 1997) – Hard to avoid the somewhat negative message here, but amid a changing culture at the BBC, the song was never banned but simply denied airtime.

Top 10 contemporary songs played at funerals

1. **'My Way'**, Frank Sinatra

2. **'Time to Say Goodbye'**, Sarah Brightman/Andrea Bocelli

3. **'Wind Beneath My Wings'**, Bette Midler

4. **'Over the Rainbow'**, Eva Cassidy

5. **'Angels'**, Robbie Williams

6. **'You Raise Me Up'**, Westlife

7. **'You'll Never Walk Alone'**, Gerry & the Pacemakers

8. **'We'll Meet Again'**, Vera Lynn

9. **'My Heart Will Go On'**, Celine Dion

10. **'Unforgettable'**, Nat King Cole

Source: The Co-operative Funeralcare, 2012, www.co-operative.coop

10 long and increasingly bizarre song titles

1 'Several Species of Small Furry Animals Gathered Together in a Cave and Grooving With a Pict' – From the album *Ummagumma* (1969) by Pink Floyd.

2 'A Huge Ever Growing Pulsating Brain That Rules From the Centre of the Ultraworld' – From the album *The Orb's Adventures Beyond the Ultraworld* (1991) by The Orb.

3 'My Cosmic Autumn Rebellion (The Inner Life as Blazing Shield of Defiance and Optimism as Celestial Spear of Action)' – From the album *At War With the Mystics* (2006) by The Flaming Lips.

4 'You Can Make Me Dance Sing or Anything (Even Take the Dog for a Walk, Mend a Fuse, Fold Away the Ironing Board, or Any Other Domestic Shortcomings)' – From the album *Snakes and Ladders* (1974) by Rod Stewart and the Faces.

5 'All Clockwork and No Bodily Fluids Makes Hal a Dull Metal Humbert / in Heaven Every Elephant Baby Wants to be So Full of Sting / Paul Simon in the Park with Canticle / But You Can't Pick Your Friends / Vacuum Genesis / DEFMACROS / HOWSOMETH / INGDOTIME / SALENGTHS / OMETHINGL / ETBFOLLOW / AAFTERNOO / NGETPRESE / NTMOMENTI / FTHINGSWO / NTALWAYSB / ETHISWAYT / BCACAUSEA / BWASTEAFT / ERNOONWHE / NEQBMERET / URNFROMSH / OWLITTLEG / REENPLACE / 27' – From the album *Lolita Nation* (1987) by Game Theory.

6 'Some People Know All Too Well How Bad Liquorice, or Any Candy for That Matter, Can Taste When Having Laid Out in the Sun Too Long – And I Think I Just Ate Too Much' – From the album *Oh Lord! When? How?* (1996) by The Hives.

7 'Sir B. McKenzie's Daughter's Lament for the 77th Mounted Lancers Retreat from the Straits of Loch Knombe, in the Year of Our Lord 1727, on the Occasion of the Announcement of Her Marriage to the Laird of Kinleakie'** – From the album *Full House* (2001, reissue) by Fairport Convention.

8 'Long Live British Democracy Which Flourishes and is Constantly Perfected Under the Immaculate Guidance of the Great, Honourable, Generous and Correct Margaret Hilda Thatcher. She is the Blue Sky in the Hearts of All Nations. Our People Pay Homage and Bow in Deep Respect and Gratitude to Her. The Milk of Human Kindness'** – From the album *A Good Night Out* (1987) by Test Department.

9 'The Sad But True Story of Ray Mingus, the Lumberjack of Bulk Rock City, and His Never Slacking Stribe in Exploiting the So Far Undiscovered Areas of the Intention to Bodily Intercourse from the Opposite Species of His Kind, During Intake of All the Mental Condition That Could be Derived from Fermentation'** – From the album *Sex and Violins* (1995) by Rednex.

10 'Regretting What I Said to You When You Called Me 11:00 On a Friday Morning to Tell Me That at 1:00 Friday Afternoon You're Gonna Leave Your Office, Go Downstairs, Hail a Cab to Go Out to the Airport to Catch a Plane to Go Skiing in the Alps for Two Weeks, Not That I Wanted to Go With You, I Wasn't Able to Leave Town, I'm Not a Very Good Skier, I Couldn't Expect You to Pay My Way, But After Going Out With You for Three Years I DON'T Like Surprises!! Subtitled: A Musical Apology'** – From the album *Future Fossils* (1994) by Christine Lavin.

10 rock star rider requests

❶ Red Hot Chili Peppers (2000) – The ageing rockers requested 'six pairs of white crew socks, 1 pair plaid cotton boxer shorts, 2 aromatherapy type candles, 24 1-litre bottles of still "glacier" wate (served at room temp), small bowls of whole, pitted dates, figs and raw, unsalted cashews and a Meditation Room (small in size).'

❷ Foo Fighters (2008) – Dave Grohl and co. kept things simple, asking for 'Eight beers (Coors light/cans), four bottles Gatorade (Remember: wacky colours please), 2 toothbrushes, 2 small hand sanitizers.' Also, 'any effort to make the dressing room comfy and sexy is much appreciated. We like to lounge about and convalesce i the dressing room. So feel free to shoplift some cool IKEA furniture.

❸ James Brown (year not stated) – The Godfather of Soul requested that rooms 'must have comfortable seating, with lights, professional hooded hair dryer, circulating fan, ironing board with steam iron'. And, 'as close to James Brown's dressing room as possible, a room must be provided for James Brown's wardrobe mistress'. Brown and his entourage 'MUST have (2) two hot meals a day'. And of course, 'there MUST be an oxygen tank and mask on stage at all times.'

❹ Iggy and The Stooges (2006) – A legendary rider, long and with its tongue firmly in cheek. Iggy requested '2 bottles of smooth, full-bodied, Bordeaux-type red wine. Probably French. And something we've heard of and still can't pronounce. Look, there's f**king loads of good red wines. Ask the man in the wine shop. 1 x case of big bottles of good, premium beer. Here's a clue – it probably won't star with a letter 'B' and end with 'udweiser'. 1 case of cans of assorted sodas. Ginger beer? Dandelion & Burdock? I don't know. Lemonade Lots and lots of clean ice. Not ice that a polar bear has been standing on, with its big mucky feet. Cauliflower/broccoli, cut into individual florets and *thrown immediately into the garbage. I f**king* **hate** *that.*' He also requested some 'fresh ginger, honey lemons and a sharp knife, so we can make ginger, honey and lemon tea. God knows why. And some Chinese gunpowder tea. So we can attempt to blow up the dressing room. That's a joke by the way. Good job this isn't an airport...'

Puff Daddy (year not stated) – Among other things, the future Diddy requested '1 gallon milk, 1 gallon of fresh squeezed orange juice, 1 gallon of apple juice, 2 bottles of Hennessy cognac, 1 bottle of Cristal champagne, 1 bottle of Dom Pérignon.'

AC/DC (2008) – Perhaps feeling their age, the hard rockers' rider requested 'small selection of imported cheeses and crackers (English cheeses and water crackers preferred), 1 box Twinings English Breakfast Tea, 50 packets of sugar'. There was '1 case of bottled Heineken', but more tellingly also '3 oxygen tanks with 3 masks that must be at the venue at load-in.'

The Beatles (1965) – Pre-global superstardom, all the Beatles asked for was a stage, 'the dimensions to be not less than 25' x 25' and at least 5' high', 'a platform for Ringo Starr and his drums' and 'four cots, mirrors, an ice cooler, portable TV set and clean towels.'

Johnny Cash (1993) – Feeling thirsty, the Man in Black requested 'Coffee – 1 gallon, milk, sugar etc, Coca-Cola Classic – 1 dozen, Spring drinking water – ½ gallon. Please – No substitutions of soft drink brands.' He also requested 'an American Flag on a pole stand (typical size 3' by 5')', to be placed 'on stage in full view of the audience throughout the show.'

DMX (2006) – A tasteful selection from the New York rapper: 'One gallon of Hennessy cognac, 24 assorted Minute Maid box juices, one pack vanilla Oreo cookies, one jar peanut butter, fresh fruit bowl (to include strawberries, assorted grapes, bananas, apples, oranges and tangerines)', plus, of course, 'three boxes of condoms (Trojan, Lifestyle or Kimono's).'

Van Halen (1982) – The most legendary rider of them all was long and contained the now infamous M&M's demand, included to make sure the venue were paying attention to the small-stuff details so that they were taking every aspect of the performance and safety seriously. The abridged version read: 'One case of Budweiser beer, four cases of Schlitz Malt Liquor beer (16 ounce cans), three-fifths Jack Daniel's Black Label bourbon, two-fifths Stolichnaya vodka, one pint Southern Comfort, two bottles of Blue Nun white wine, herring in sour cream, one (1) large tube KY Jelly and M&M's (WARNING: ABSOLUTELY NO BROWN ONES).'

Source: The Smoking Gun, www.thesmokinggun.com

These are heavily excerpted versions of the full riders, which can be seen in their entirety at www.thesmokinggun.com.

10 insured celebrity body parts

1. **Gene Simmons' tongue** – Reportedly insured for $1 million

2. **Basil Brush's tail** – £1 million

3. **Keith Richards' hands** – $1.6 million–2 million

4. **Kylie Minogue's buttocks** – $5 million

5. **Dolly Parton's breasts** – $600,000 for the pair, $300,000 apiece

6. **Daniel Craig's body** – (Insured against injury during the filming of *Quantum of Solace*) $9.5 million

7. **Egon Ronay's tastebuds** – $400,000

8. **Cristiano Ronaldo's legs** – $144 million

9. **Comedian Rich Hall's sense of humour** – (Insured against loss of) £1 million

10. **Tom Jones' chest hair** – $7 million

10 famous people who changed their names

1 **Bruce Willis** was **Walter Willison** (Bruce was his middle name)

2 **Woody Allen** was **Allen Konigsberg**

3 **Malcolm X** was **Malcolm Little**

4 **Chevy Chase** was **Cornelius Chase**

5 **Michael Caine** was **Maurice Micklewhite**

6 **Hulk Hogan** was **Terry Jean Bollette**

7 **Stevie Wonder** was **Steveland Hardaway Judkins**

8 **Ben Kingsley** was **Krishna Pandit Bhanji**

9 **Christopher Walken** was **Ronald Walken**

10 **River Phoenix** was **River Bottom**

10 famous people who declined British honours

1 **David Bowie** – Recording artist, declined a CBE in the Queen's Birthday Honours of 2000.

2 **Nigella Lawson** – Celebrity cook, rejected a 2001 OBE for services to journalism and to cookery.

3 **Roald Dahl** – Children's author, turned down an OBE in 1986.

4 **Bernie Ecclestone** – Formula One controller, turned down a CBE for services to motor racing in 1996.

5 **Danny Boyle** – London 2012 opening ceremony mastermind, turned down a knighthood in 2012 in recognition of his services to Britain.

6 **Dawn French and Jennifer Saunders** – Comedy duo, turned down 2001 OBEs for services to comedy drama.

7 **L. S. Lowry** – Painter, reportedly turned down five awards, including a knighthood, CBE and OBE.

8 **Albert Finney** – Actor, rejected a knighthood in 2000 and a CBE in 1980.

9 **Alfred Hitchcock** – Film director, reportedly rejected a CBE in 1962 but accepted a knighthood in 1980.

10 **John Lennon** – Recording artist, returned his MBE in 1969 'in protest against Britain's involvement in the Nigeria-Biafra thing, against our support of America in Vietnam and against [his single] "Cold Turkey" slipping down the charts'.

Source: The British government's Cabinet Office

10 celebrities qualified to fly

Tom Cruise – Earned his private pilot's licence in 1994, having caught the bug filming *Top Gun*. Owns and pilots several aircraft, including a Gulfstream GIV.

Clint Eastwood – A licensed pilot for more than three decades and still flying into his seventies, Eastwood prefers to pilot helicopters over planes.

Bruce Dickinson – The most dedicated celebrity pilot on this list, the Iron Maiden frontman has spent 20 years as a charter pilot, during which time he's clocked up well over 7,000 hours of flying time.

Harrison Ford – After piloting the *Millennium Falcon*, anything else will seem easy. Originally trained in the 1960s, Ford is said to be fond of the De Havilland Canada DHC-2 Beaver seaplane.

Angelina Jolie – A qualified pilot since 2004, Jolie has been said to occasionally fly barefoot and been seen piloting a Cirrus SR22, which has a top speed of 480 km/h (300 mph).

Morgan Freeman – Despite once being employed as an Air Force mechanic, Freeman only learned to fly aged 65. He reportedly owns a $6.9 million Sino Swearingen SJ30 business jet.

Phil Mickelson – One of several golf star pilots, Mickelson followed in the footsteps of his former navy and airline pilot father and now owns a Gulfstream G550.

Gisele Bündchen – Leggy supermodel, became a qualified helicopter pilot in 2009, taking her tests while pregnant. Said to favour helicopters over planes.

Dave Lee Roth – The Van Halen frontman gained his private pilot licence for rotorcraft helicopters in 2006. Insert your own 'nice chopper' line here, before he inevitably does.

Patrick Swayze – The star of *Dirty Dancing* was a highly skilled pilot, and once expertly brought his Cessna down in a Las Vegas suburb during an emergency landing.

10 memorable misbehaving celebrities

1 **Bill Murray** – Having been stopped driving a golf buggy through the centre of Stockholm in 2007, the Hollywood grouch was taken to Norrmalm police station after refusing to take a breath test. He later admitted that drink had been taken.

2 **Matthew McConaughey** – Police called to McConaughey's Texas home in 1999 discovered the Hollywood hunk stark-bollock naked and playing the bongo drums. Charged with possession of marijuana and drug paraphernalia, the drug charges were dropped

3 **Gérard Depardieu** – Famously caught urinating in the aisle on board a flight in 2011, the following year a motorist filed a complaint against the French thespian, accusing Depardieu of punching him after Depardieu's scooter allegedly collided with the unnamed driver's vehicle.

4 **John Daly** – The troubled golfer passed out in a branch of Hooters restaurant after a bout of heavy drinking in 2008. Attempting to rouse him, police found him dangerously drunk and uncooperative, so took him into custody to sober up.

5 **Christian Slater** – In 1994, the *True Romance* actor thought it was acceptable to carry a gun through an airport. Even before post-9/11 panic set in, officers at New York's JFK airport begged to differ. His punishment saw him working with homeless kids for three days.

Nick Nolte – The actor was arrested by California Highway Patrol for driving under the influence in 2002. That in itself is not remarkable, he's hardly Hollywood's first DUI, but his mugshot really is: Nolte's crazy hair and Hawaiian shirt make him look like a terrifyingly intoxicated Joker.

George Clooney – Arrested during a 2012 protest outside the Sudanese Embassy in Washington, Clooney was given three verbal warnings not to cross a police line before being carted off in handcuffs. He was released after a few hours in custody, having paid a $100 fine.

Bill Gates – Prior to becoming a multi-billionaire philanthropist, the future Microsoft founder was arrested for a traffic violation in Albuquerque, New Mexico in 1977, two years after being arrested for speeding and driving without a valid licence.

Paul McCartney – Flying into Japan with his other band, Wings, in 1980, McCartney received two thumbs down when customs officials discovered he was carrying about 200 g (7 oz) of cannabis. They kept him in jail for ten days before deporting him without charge.

Rip Torn – With previous arrests for drunk-driving, the US actor hit a new low in 2010 by breaking into a closed bank in Connecticut while carrying a gun. So inebriated was the 78-year-old, he believed he was at home and so left his hat and boots by the door. He narrowly avoided a jail sentence.

10 final resting places of the rich and famous

1 **Frank Sinatra**, singer/actor (1915-98), is buried in Desert Memorial Park (Cathedral City, California, USA)

2 **Jim Morrison**, rock star (1943-71), is buried in Père Lachaise Cemetery (Paris, France)

3 **James Dean**, actor (1931-55), is buried in Park Cemetery (Fairmoun Indiana, USA)

4 **Princess Diana**, 'Queen Of Our Hearts' (1961-97), is buried in the grounds of Althorp Estate (Northamptonshire, UK)

5 **Michael Jackson**, pop star (1958-2009), is buried in Great Mausoleum, Forest Lawn (Glendale, Los Angeles, USA)

6 **Sir Isaac Newton**, scientist (1642-1727), is buried in Westminster Abbey (London, UK)

7 **Bruce Lee**, martial artist (1940-73), is buried in Lakeview Cemetery (Seattle, Washington, USA)

8 **The Krays**, criminals (Ronnie 1933-95; Reggie 1933-2000), are buried in Chingford Mount Cemetery (Chingford, Essex, UK)

9 **William Shakespeare**, 'The Bard of Avon' (1564-1616), is buried in Holy Trinity Churchyard (Stratford-upon-Avon, Warwickshire, UK)

10 **Winston Churchill**, prime minister (1874-1965), is buried in the Churchill family plot, St Martin's Church (Bladon, Oxfordshire, UK)

10 classic comic one-liners

1 'I want to die like my father, peacefully in his sleep, not screaming and terrified, like his passengers.' – Bob Monkhouse

2 'A girl phoned me the other day and said, "Come on over, there's nobody home." I went over. Nobody was home.' – Rodney Dangerfield

3 'Two elephants walk off a cliff ... boom, boom!' – Tommy Cooper

4 'I was walking in the park and this guy waved at me. Then he said, "I'm sorry, I thought you were someone else." I said, "I am".' – Demetri Martin

5 'My wife sent her photograph to the Lonely Hearts Club. They sent it back saying they weren't that lonely.' – Les Dawson

6 'I don't think my wife likes me very much, when I had a heart attack she wrote for an ambulance.' – Frank Carson

7 'I can whistle with my fingers, especially if I have a whistle.' – Mitch Hedberg

8 'I never forget a face, but in your case I'd be glad to make an exception.' – Groucho Marx

9 'My friend drowned in a bowl of muesli. A strong currant pulled him in.' – Tommy Cooper

10 'I can still enjoy sex at 74 – I live at 75, so it's no distance.' – Bob Monkhouse

10 bizarre celebrity endorsements

1 **Louis Vuitton bags** – Once one of the world's most powerful men and the last leader of the Soviet Union, Mikhail Gorbachev put his name and face to Louis Vuitton luggage.

2 **The Flavorwave Turbo Oven** – A miracle of modern cooking, producing juicier fare in a fraction of the time through halogen heat, infrared waves and convection cooking, brought to you in association with the actor and one-time nightclub bouncer, Mr T.

3 **The Kiss Kasket** – A $4,700 coffin emblazoned with images of the band Kiss, the weirdest in a wide arsenal of products plugged that also includes condoms, credit cards and pinball machines.

4 **Hertz Car Rentals** – O. J. Simpson's endorsement of the car rental firm took on extra significance when the former American football star took off down the LA freeway with several LAPD cars in hot pursuit. Luckily for Hertz, it wasn't one of their automobiles.

5 **Gold** – MC Hammer, the one-time baggy-panted pop rap prince, must have fallen on hard times, fronting an ad in which he tells how he's trading in his unwanted gold – gold sledge hammer, gold Hammer pants, gold discs – for cash, via Cash4Gold.com.

6 **Chocolate** – Michael Jackson made ends meet by putting his name and face to a range of premium Swiss chocolate. Staring down from the packaging like some self-appointed Willy Wonka, Jackson's creepy visage could make a child lose his appetite.

7 **Beer –** When old 'Slow Hand', Eric Clapton, was endorsing Michelob beer, he was also battling alcoholism, so it was an odd fit. When the sorry truth came out, the campaign was quickly pulled.

8 **Smokey Robinson's Down Home Pot Roast** – The R&B legend Smokey Robinson did more than endorse this delicious-sounding frozen ready-meal – his company, SFGL, was responsible for concocting and selling the stuff, alongside Smokey Robinson's Chicken and Sausage Gumbo. 'The soul is in the bowl,' he chirped.

9 **Butter** – Ozzy Osbourne went from biting the heads off bats to peddling I Can't Believe It's Not Butter, in one simple pay cheque. More recently, of course, old punk John Lydon has pulled a similar stunt, advertising Country Life butter.

10 **Fortified wine** – Hindsight is a wonderful thing, but Pope Leo XIII might today regret putting his celebrity name to Vin Mariani in the mid to late 19th century. Wildly popular back then, it was laced with cocaine and would go on to inspire the creation of Coca-Cola.

Top 10 most popular apps*

	IPHONE (PAID)	IPAD (PAID)	IPHONE (FREE)	IPAD (FREE)
1	Angry Birds	Pages	Facebook	Skype
2	Fruit Ninja	Angry Birds	Pandora Radio	The Weather Channel
3	Doodle Jump	Angry Birds Seasons	Instagram	Netflix
4	Cut the Rope	Where's My Water	YouTube	Angry Birds Free
5	Angry Birds Seasons	Fruit Ninja	Skype	Kindle
6	WhatsApp Messenger	Angry Birds Space	Words With Friends	Facebook
7	Camera+	GarageBand	The Weather Channel	Pandora Radio
8	Words With Friends	Words With Friends	Twitter	Calculator
9	Tiny Wings	Cut the Rope	Temple Run	Fruit Ninja
10	Angry Birds Space	Keynote	Google Search	Words With Friends

*Apple apps as at 2 May 2013

Source: Apple

The figures for most popular apps were released by Apple to coincide with the five-year anniversary of the iOS App Store.

Top 10 most popular websites*

IN THE WORLD

IN THE UK

1 **www.google.com**
(search engine)

www.google.co.uk
(search engine)

2 **www.facebook.com**
(social networking)

www.google.com
(search engine)

3 **www.youtube.com**
(video sharing)

www.facebook.com
(social networking)

4 **www.yahoo.com**
(search engine)

www.youtube.com
(video sharing)

5 **www.baidu.com**
(Chinese search engine)

www.ebay.co.uk
(online auction)

6 **www.wikipedia.org**
(online encyclopedia)

www.bbc.co.uk
(broadcaster website)

7 **www.qq.com**
(Chinese internet portal)

www.amazon.co.uk
(online marketplace)

8 **www.amazon.com**
(online marketplace)

www.yahoo.com
(search engine)

9 **www.live.com**
(Microsoft search engine)

www.wikipedia.org
(online encyclopedia)

0 **www.taobao.com**
(Chinese online marketplace)

www.linkedin.com
(business networking)

*Ranking correct as at December 2013. The list is based on the Alexa Traffic Rank which measures how a website is doing relative to all other sites on the web over the past three months, calculated using a combination of the estimated average daily unique visitors to the site and the estimated number of pageviews on the site. The site with the highest combination of unique visitors and pageviews is ranked No. 1.

Source: Alexa, the leading provider of free, global web metrics. © 2013, Alexa Internet, www.alexa.com

10 defining moments of Twitter

1 **'Just setting up my twttr' @jack** – Twitter's first ever tweet, posted on 21 March 2006 by the company's co-creator, Jack Dorsey.

2 **'From orbit: Launch was awesome!! I am feeling great, working hard, & enjoying the magnificent views, the adventure of a lifetime has begun!' @astro_mike** – NASA astronaut Mike Massimino sends the historic first tweet from space, May 2009.

3 **'I just watched a plane crash into the hudson rive [sic] in manhattan' @highfours** – The first recorded tweet about the crash of a US Airways jet into New York's Hudson River in 2009, confirming Twitter's ability to break news stories far quicker than traditional news sources. Images quickly followed.

4 **'We regretfully admit that something has happened off of the Gulf Coast. More to come.' @BPGlobalPR** – Spoof account set up in the immediate aftermath of the Deepwater Horizon oil disaster in the Gulf of Mexico in April 2010, reflecting BP's alleged lack of concern. A second tweet quickly followed that read: 'Adorable! Naughty Kitty Makes a Mess! http://www.youtube.com/watch?v=greOQOD6GDA.'

5 **'Everest summit! -Sent with @DeLorneGPS Earthmate PN-60w' @ELexplore** – In October 2010, American explorer Eric Larsen became the first man to officially tweet the world from the summit of Mount Everest, with obligatory mention for the providers of his technical gadgetry.

'Here r the latest updates: The govt is countermobilizing against us now. There r several pro-Mubarak protests taking place in Cairo now.' @3arabawy – One of the first tweets to come out of Egypt on 2 February 2011, as the 'Egyptian Uprising' unfolded. What followed was described by many as the first Twitter revolution.

'Millions are in uproar in #Cairo. Rumor is they heard our new spring collection is now available' @KennethCole – US fashion label Kenneth Cole misjudges the mood in February 2011, attempting to promote its new spring collection amid Egyptian bloodshed. It is inevitably greeted by a Twittersphere backlash of disapproval.

'Dear friends, I am pleased to get in touch with you through Twitter. Thank you for your generous response. I bless all of you from my heart.' @Pontifex – Reportedly sent from the papal iPad, Pope Benedict XVI posts his very first tweet, 12 December 2012.

'Helicopter hovering above Abbottabad at 1AM (is a rare event).' @ReallyVirtual – In May 2011, a Pakistani IT consultant suddenly found himself unwittingly updating the world on Navy Seals storming the compound of Osama bin Laden and killing the world's most wanted man.

'Be on the look for DSS041GP my boyufriend [sic] has just been hijacked and is in the boot please RT.' @onebadvillynn – In April 2012, a kidnapped man bundled into the boot of a car texted his girlfriend. She tweeted the world, the car was swiftly tracked down and her boyfriend saved. Why he didn't just call the police from the boot of the car is not the point here: Twitter saves lives.

Top 10 biggest-selling computer games of all time

TECHNOLOGY

GAME/YEAR	PLATFORM	TOTAL GLOBAL SALES*
❶ *Wii Sports* (2006)	Nintendo Wii	81.4 million
❷ *Super Mario Bros.* (1985)	Nintendo Entertainment System	40.24 million
❸ *Mario Kart Wii* (2008)	Nintendo Wii	33.81 million
❹ *Wii Sports Resort* (2009)	Nintendo Wii	31.81 million
❺ *Pokémon: Red/Green/ Blue Versions* (1996)	Nintendo Game Boy	31.37 million
❻ *Tetris* (1989)	Nintendo Game Boy	30.26 million
❼ *New Super Mario Bros.* (2006)	Nintendo DS	29.11 million
❽ *Wii Play* (2006)	Nintendo Wii	28.73 million
❾ *Duck Hunt* (1984)	Nintendo Entertainment System	28.31 million
❿ *New Super Mario Bros.* (2009)	Nintendo Wii	26.82 million

*In millions of units per game as at November 2013

Source: VGChartz, www.vgchartz.com

The first non-Nintendo title to appear on the bestsellers list comes in at number 16: *Grand Theft Auto: San Andreas* on the PS2, released in 2004 by Take-Two Interactive, with global sales of 20.81 million.

Top 10 most influential computer games ever made*

Doom (1993, PC) – Science fiction, horror-themed, first-person shoot-em-up, repelling wave after wave of demons from hell. Top because: 'Nothing will ever quite achieve the original *Doom*'s impact.'

Pac-Man (1980, Arcade) – Ravenous yellow pill muncher, pursued by ghosts. 'Graphics can come and go, but a good addictive gameplay mechanic never dies.'

World of Warcraft (2004, PC) – Multiplayer, online, real-time, role-playing epic. 'WoW wasn't the first of its line, just the best realized.'

The Legend of Zelda: Ocarina of Time (1998, N64) – Action-adventure epic, starring the intrepid Link. This spawned 'a game series of near incalculable reach.'

Spacewar! (1962, PDP-1) – Rudimentary but revolutionary two-player space combat game. 'It's hard to think of a game with more far-reaching influence than *Spacewar!*'

Tomb Raider (1996, Saturn) – Indiana Jones-inspired epic, starring woman with impractically large breasts. 'Few would deny that gaming's first heroine (unless you count Ms. Pac-Man) had a lasting impact on how videogames were popularly perceived.'

Tetris (1984, various platforms) – An exercise in box stacking. 'Now, 30 years after it first challenged the minds, and thumbs, of devoted players, *Tetris* has lost none of its playability.'

Super Mario 64 (1996, N64) – Moustachioed plumber's platform adventure. 'A game-changer in the platform genre.'

StarCraft (1998, PC) – Military strategy game. 'Impossible to overestimate ... every real time strategy game since lives in *StarCraft*'s shadow.'

Civilization (1991, PC) – A turn-based strategy classic, set initially in the year 4000BC. 'The sheer scale of *Civilization*'s ambition is hard to beat.'

---

*According to *Stuff* magazine

Source and quotes: *Stuff* magazine, www.stuff.tv

10 controversial computer games

1 *Death Race* (1976) – Twee now but a corrupting influence back in 1976: in *Death Race* you drove a rudimentary 'car' down the screen and received points by driving over gremlins – which looked more like humans, and cried out in anguish. Odd also that the game's name had been changed from *Pedestrian*.

2 *Mortal Kombat* (1992) – At the time the most realistic fighting game around, *Mortal Kombat* kicked up a stink by becoming the first to introduce fighter fatalities – players were soon able to rip off their opponent's head and pull out his still-beating heart.

3 *Doom* (1993) – Our first introduction to the new genre of First Person Shooter, *Doom*'s heavy dose of blood, guts and gore had already pricked the ears of Middle America's moral majority. When it transpired the perpetrators of the Columbine High School massacre were avid fans, their outrage went into overdrive.

4 *Tomb Raider* (1996) – An admirable and in many ways pioneering action adventure which saw, through no fault of the publishers, devious little perverts concoct a thoroughly despicable 'patch', nicknamed 'Nude Raider'. It allowed fans to play as a naked Lara Croft.

5 *Grand Theft Auto* (1997) – Perhaps the most controversial title in gaming history, the original *GTA* allowed kids to play a criminal on the streets of a fictional city, robbing, looting and callously shooting for personal gain. It's since spawned five sequels, each garnering equal parts outrage and acclaim.

6 *The Sims 2* (2000) – Strategic 'life simulator' game, featuring pretend people engaged in a series of real life scenarios. Controversy hit the title when it became possible to modify the game to include sexually explicit images – or in the words of one raging US attorney, to portray 'labia, nipples, pubic hair and penises

7 **Dead or Alive Xtreme Beach Volleyball** (2003) – In a significant departure from the usual *DoA* fighting franchise, Japanese games house Tecmo released a beach volleyball title that became less celebrated for its game play than for the array of scantily clad young ladies who bent over a lot. It featured a zoom option. Feminist outrage predictably ensued.

8 **Postal 2** (2003) – Created to cause maximum controversy, *Postal 2* took its title from the act of 'going postal', inviting idiots to decapitate police officers, librarians, innocent people standing in the queue and some cats, before urinating on the corpses. Helpfully, the amount of urine dispensed was kept on a sadistic statistics page.

9 **Manhunt** (2003) – Brought to us by the brains behind *GTA*, *Manhunt* took brutality to a whole new level. The introduction to the game saw the 'star', James Earl Cash, pull a plastic bag over a gang member's head, suffocating him before snapping his neck. The scene for the rest of the game was very much set and it spawned an equally unpleasant sequel.

10 **Call of Duty: Modern Warfare 2** (2009) – A combat series that had already caused controversy for its bloodthirsty content, *Modern Warfare 2* courted condemnation by offering a level where the player switched to the terrorist's side and gunned down innocent civilians in an airport. It didn't help that the game was released around the time of 13 people being shot dead at Fort Hood in Texas.

10 real people with remarkable names

1 **Randy Shoemaker** – Iowan professor studying the genetic map of soya beans

2 **Mustafa Koc** – Businessman, chairman of Koc Holding

3 **Yolanda Squatpump** – American make-up artist, worked on the film *The Usual Suspects*

4 **Jesus Ponce** – Mexican footballer, played for Guadalajara in the 1970s

5 **Gyant Shitole** – Incongruously named banker from the paradise island of Mauritius

6 **Mary Christmas** – One of three women tracked down by the *Daily Mirror* in 2009

7 **William Pancake** – Eighth-century resident of Pennsylvania

8 **Mercedes Carr** – Ohio-based healthcare professional

9 **Bongo Christ** – Congolese footballer, played for a variety of clubs including Hannover 96; retired in 2008

10 **Tony Bollock** – Founder of the US Lafayette-based Bollock Industries, 'Custom Countertops and Closet Organizers Since 1960'

Source: The Daft Name Directory, twitter.com/daftnames

The above are all real people saddled with 'colourful' monikers – none of which were changed by deed poll.

10 more real people with remarkable names

1 **Norman Conquest** – Australia's hapless goalkeeper in the 17-0 defeat to England in 1951

2 **Cliff Hanger** – Works in Burger King on the M1 near East Midlands Airport

3 **Crescent Dragonwagon**– Award-winning US food writer, can be found blogging at www.dragonwagon.com

4 **Danger Fourpence** – Zimbabwean footballer

5 **Professor Reinhardt Adolfo Fuck** – Brazilian geology boffin, once of Durham University

6 **Samson Dutch Boy Gym** – Super flyweight boxer from Thailand, retired undefeated in 2002

7 **Fanny Horn** – Norwegian female biathlete

8 **Taco Monster** – Dutch pharmacoepidemiologist

9 **Johnny Moustache** – Footballer who played one game for Seychelles as a striker in 2000, and sported a goatee

10 **Tokyo Sexwale –** Minister of Human Settlement in the South African government

Source: The Daft Name Directory, twitter.com/daftnames

Top 10 most popular baby names in Britain*

NAMES

	1914	1964	2012
1	John and Mary	David and Susan	Harry and Amelia
2	William and Margaret	Paul and Julie	Oliver and Olivia
3	George and Doris	Andrew and Karen	Jack and Jessica
4	Thomas and Dorothy	Mark and Jacqueline	Charlie and Emily
5	James and Kathleen	John and Deborah	Jacob and Lily
6	Arthur and Florence	Michael and Tracey	Thomas and Ava
7	Frederick and Elsie	Stephen and Jane	Alfie and Mia
8	Albert and Edith	Ian and Helen	Riley and Isla
9	Charles and Elizabeth	Robert and Diane	William and Sophie
10	Robert and Winifred	Richard and Sharon	James and Isabella

*Names registered in England and Wales

Source: The Office for National Statistics, www.ons.gov.uk

10 'unconventional' names for celebrities' kids

1 **Zuma Nesta Rock Rossdale** – The son of peroxide pop princess Gwen Stefani and her seemingly retired husband Gavin Rossdale.

2 **Audio Science Clayton** – The son of *A Knight's Tale* actress Shannyn Sossamon and children's book illustrator Dallas Clayton.

3 **Buddy Bear Maurice Oliver** – The son of Jamie Oliver and Jools Oliver, a brother to Poppy Honey, Daisy Boo and Petal.

4 **Jermajesty Jackson** – The son of Jermaine Jackson and Alejandra Oaziaza, proving Michael didn't have a monopoly on the weirdness.

5 **Moon Unit Zappa** – Daughter of rock star Frank and his wife Gail, sister to Diva Muffin and Dweezil.

6 **Ignatius Martin Upton** – The son of Australian actress Cate Blanchett and her director husband Andrew Upton.

7 **Moroccan Scott Cannon** – The daughter of pop diva Mariah Carey and actor, rapper and comedian Nick Cannon. She's neither Moroccan or Scottish, or indeed a cannon, but supposedly named after the African styling in Carey's New York apartment.

8 **Bronx Mowgli Wentz** – The son of unashamed *Jungle Book* fans Ashlee Simpson (the actress) and Pete Wentz (the rock star).

9 **Bear Blu** – The son of actress Alicia Silverstone and musician Christopher Jarecki, who haven't considered that their boy will one day be a pensioner.

10 **Pilot Inspektor Riesgraf Lee** – The improbably named son of *My Name is Earl* star Jason Lee and actress Beth Riesgraf.

The 10 sexiest women of the last decade

NAME	YEAR
1 Mila Kunis	2013
2 Tulisa	2012
3 Rosie Huntington-Whiteley	2011
4 Cheryl Cole	2010
5 Cheryl Cole	2009
6 Megan Fox	2008
7 Jessica Alba	2007
8 Kiera Knightley	2006
9 Kelly Brook	2005
10 Britney Spears	2004

Source: *FHM* magazine

In 2014, *FHM* celebrates the 20th anniversary of the *FHM* '100 Sexiest Women in the World' list.

10 unexpected condom flavours

1 **Garlic** – Available via renowned garlic-themed restaurant The Stinking Rose.

2 **Bacon** – J&D's bacon-flavoured condoms, 'lubricated with baconlube™'. Mmm.

3 **Durian fruit** – An odd inspiration given this fruit native to South-east Asia is banned in some countries on account of its obnoxious stench.

4 **Scotch whisky** – Very proudly and patriotically brought to you by a manufacturer called McCondom.

5 **Coffee** – Brought to you by Scalex. Milk? Sugar? Sadly, they don't say.

6 **Bubblegum** – 'Blow Me Bubblegum Flavoured', to be exact, brought to you by Skins.

7 **Fizzy cola** – The 'EXS Crazy Cola' condom from the truly pioneering 'EXS Taste the Difference Range'.

8 **Blueberry muffin** – Blueberry is popular in the world of flavoured condoms. EXS goes a step further with its cake-themed offering.

9 **Hot chocolate** – A third from the extensive 'EXS Taste the Difference Range', which also includes orange soda and strawberry sundae.

10 **Cannabis inspired** – Brought to you, if you're that way inclined, by condom company Blowdom.

Top 10 most popular sex products*

1 **Lovehoney Jessica Rabbit 2.0 Rabbit Vibrator** – 'Combines vibrating rabbit ears with an exquisite swirling beaded shaft to give double stimulation.'

2 **Sqweel 2 Oral Sex Simulator** – 'Features a wheel with 10 lapping silicone tongues, 3 powerful speeds, 30% more power and a new reversible mode and flicker function.'

3 **Lovehoney BASICS Anal Douche** – 'One step insertion and maximum cleansing. Features a glow in the dark tip to show you the way.'

4 **Lovehoney BASICS Slimline Butt Buddy Butt Plug** – 'Ideal for beginners or those who want an easy-to-use plug which sits comfortably for hour after pleasurable hour.'

5 **Lovehoney Powerful Pocket Vibrator** – 'Small but mighty, four interchangeable heads ... ideal for beginners and at a loveable price.'

6 **Tracey Cox Supersex Bullet Vibrator** – 'Small enough to take anywhere but strong enough to deliver intense vibrations whenever you need it.'

7 **Lovehoney BASICS Smoothy Anal Prober** – 'Use the graduated beads side to start with, then try the smooth tapered side to build up to more fulfilling experience.'

8 **Lovehoney Mains Powered Deluxe Magic Wand Vibrator** – 'With a wide head and flexible neck, this massager vibrator gives incredible sensations.'

9 **Lovehoney 10 Function Remote Control Dream Egg** – 'Offering 3 speeds and 7 patterns ... powered by a remote for fun in and out of the bedroom.'

10 **Lovehoney BASICS Oriental Ben Wa Jiggle Balls** – 'Simply insert and take a walk. Each sphere houses a small ball that wiggles when you do, resulting in sensational stimulation.'

*Based on sales of products sold between 2008 and 2013 at leading online adult sex toy company Lovehoney

Source: Lovehoney, www.lovehoney.co.uk.

10 supposedly aphrodisiac foods

1 **Aniseed** – Favoured by the ancient Romans and Greeks, who sucked on seeds because they didn't have ouzo. The seed's estrogenic compounds will supposedly produce a rapid spike in your sex drive.

2 **Bananas** – Celebrated for their high levels of potassium and B vitamins, both of which are said to benefit sex hormone production. And, on a very base level, the shape also triggers 'mucky thoughts'.

3 **Caviar** – Their high levels of zinc are said to increase the production of testosterone, which aids sexual stimulation. However, with them being fish eggs and all, do eat a mint afterwards.

4 **Chilli peppers** – Hotter peppers are considered aphrodisiacal for their ability to cause sweating and increase heart rate and circulation – mimicking the sensations experienced during the act of 'doing it'.

5 **Chocolate** – High levels of phenylethylamine and theobromine help produce a sense of wellbeing and increase feelings of sexy pleasure. It's more evident in dark chocolate with a high cocoa content than in a Kit Kat Chunky, for example, but you can experiment.

6 **Oysters** – A celebrated penile pick-me-up dating back to the Romans, who believed that the high levels of zinc and amino acids in oysters would trigger the production of sex hormones.

7 **Garlic** – A problematic predicament, here. Garlic contains an amino acid that enhances circulation, increases blood flow and helps put a little more lead in your pencil. But on the flip side, you will stink and she won't want to kiss you.

8 **Avocado** – An aphrodisiac either because of the high levels of vitamin E, or because they resemble your 'swingers' – the Aztecs called the avocado tree a 'testicle tree', for they hang in pairs.

9 **Pumpkin seeds** – High in magnesium, which produces greater blood flow and helps raise testosterone levels.

10 **Horny goat weed** – A thick, green, herby weed that supposedly increased sexual activity in a flock of Chinese goats after they gorged themselves on it. Now available in pill form from all good health-food stores.

Top 10 baby-producing months in Britain

MONTH	BIRTHS*
1 July	60,000
2 August	58,771
3 October	58,604
4 September	58,049
5 December	57,992
6 June	57,942
7 May	57,852
8 November	57,575
9 January	57,263
10 March	56,796

*For 2011 (latest year for which figures are available)
Source: The Royal College of Midwives

10 very brief celebrity marriages

DURATION	COUPLE/YEAR
1 **55 hours**	Britney Spears and Jason Alexander (2004)
2 **8 days**	Dennis Hopper and Michelle Phillips (1970)
3 **9 days**	Dennis Rodman and Carmen Electra (1998)
4 **16 days**	Sinead O'Connor and Barry Herridge (2011)
5 **60 days (approx.)**	Pamela Anderson and Rick Salomon (2007)
6 **72 days**	Kim Kardashian and Kris Humphries (2013)
7 **107 days**	Nicolas Cage and Lisa-Marie Presley (2002)
8 **120 days (approx.)**	Bradley Cooper and Jennifer Esposito (2006)
9 **122 days**	Pamela Anderson and Kid Rock (2006)
10 **218 days**	Jennifer Lopez and Cris Judd (2001)

10 facts about the average man

1 He stands 1.78 m (5 ft 10 in) tall and weighs 79.4 kg (175 lb).

2 He will spend 10,585 hours (441 days) in the pub in his lifetime.

3 He will sit for 11 years on his backside in front of the television.

4 He will learn to cook just four meals in his lifetime, one of which is spaghetti Bolognese.

5 He will have slept with nine partners by the time he dies.

6 Over the course of his lifetime, he'll waste a full month looking for his socks.

7 During the course of his life, he will apologize 1.9 million times.

8 Each year he spends £570 on clothes, £1,144 on beer, £2,189 on gadgets and £417 on eating out.

9 On the delicate subject of penis size, when standing proud, the average measures between 14 and 16 cm (5.5 and 6.3 in).

10 And he will die aged 78.66 (compared with the average woman, who lives to be 82.64), which is up from 71.75 in 1985.

Source: Kelkoo, www.kelkoo.com (Nos. 1–8, figures published 2011); www.nhs.uk (No. 9, published 2013); www.ons.gov.uk (No. 10, published 2013)

10 facts about the human body

1 **The smallest bone in the body is the 'stirrup'** – Found deep in the ear and hardly larger than a grain of rice.

2 **The ears and end of the nose contain no bones** – Their inner supports are cartilage or 'gristle', which is lighter and more flexible than bone, which is why the nose and ears can be bent.

3 **Smiling is easier than frowning** – There are about 60 muscles in the face and it takes 20 muscles to smile but more than 40 to frown.

4 **A man's heart will beat around 3 billion times in his lifetime** – This is the number of heartbeats for the average man living into his late seventies.

5 **It takes about one minute for a red blood cell to circle the whole body** – Each red blood cell may live for up to four months and makes approximately 250,000 round trips of the body before returning to the bone marrow, where they were born, to die.

6 **Brain cells cannot regenerate** – Unlike other body cells, once your brain cells are damaged they cannot be replaced.

7 **Around 1.5 litres (2.6 pints) of saliva are produced a day** – Saliva helps facilitate speech, mastication and swallowing while also protecting your teeth.

8 **At rest, the adult body takes in and breathes out about 6 litres (10.6 pints) of air a minute** – The breathing rate at rest is usually between 12 and 15 breaths a minute, though this is slightly faster in women and children.

9 **Muscles contract in waves to move food down the oesophagus** – This means that food would reach your stomach, even if you were standing on your head.

10 **The surface area of the lungs is roughly the same size as the area of a tennis court.**

Source: www.bodyworlds.com, Institute for Plastination, Heidelberg, Germany

Top 10 UK places where men live longest

LIFE & DEATH

LOCATION	LIFE EXPECTANCY AT BIRTH*
1 **East Dorset** (South West)	83
2 **Hart (district)** (South East)	82.6
3 **South Cambridgeshire** (East of England)	82.1
4 **Brentwood** (East of England)	82
=5 **Epsom and Ewell** (South East)	81.9
=5 **Rutland** (East Midlands)	81.9
=5 **Guildford** (South East)	81.9
=8 **Elmbridge** (South East)	81.8
=8 **New Forest** (South East)	81.8
=8 **North Dorset** (South West)	81.8

*For the period 2009–11; latest available figures as at July 2013

Source: Office for National Statistics, www.ons.gov.uk

The 10 UK places where men die soonest

LOCATION	LIFE EXPECTANCY AT BIRTH*
1 Blackpool (North West)	73.8
2 Manchester (North West)	74
3 Salford (North West)	75.6
3 Burnley (North West)	75.6
5 Liverpool (North West)	75.7
6 Blackburn with Darwen (North West)	75.7
7 Middlesbrough (North East)	75.8
7 Hyndburn (North West)	75.8
7 Rhondda Cynon Taf (Wales)	75.8
10 Tameside (North West)	75.9

*For the period 2009–11; latest available figures as at July 2013
Source: Office for National Statistics, www.ons.gov.uk

LIFE & DEATH

The 10 main causes of male deaths in the UK

CAUSE OF DEATH	REGISTERED MALE DEATHS*	PERCENTAGE OF TOTAL MALE DEATH
1 **Heart disease**	37,423	15.6
2 **Lung cancer**	16,698	
3 **Emphysema/bronchitis**	14,378	6
4 **Stroke**	14,116	5.9
5 **Dementia and Alzheimer's**	13,984	5.8
6 **Flu/pneumonia**	11,063	4.6
7 **Prostate cancer**	9,698	4
8 **Bowel cancer**	7,841	3.3
9 **Lymphoid cancer**	6,301	2.6
10 **Throat cancer**	4,603	1.9

*2012 figures for England and Wales

Source: Office for National Statistics, www.ons.gov.uk

10 accidental ways we die

ACCIDENT	REGISTERED DEATHS*	
	MALE	FEMALE
Fall from a ladder	51	1
Fall from a tree	6	0
Fall from a cliff	5	5
Contact with hot water tap	1	0
Drowning in bath	7	9
Bitten or struck by dog	5	1
Contact with venomous snakes and lizards	1	0
Choking on food	122	88
Accidental suffocation while in bed	3	5
Foreign body entering into or through eye or natural orifice	6	3

*2011 figures

Source: Office for National Statistics, www.ons.gov.uk

These are not the ten most common accidental ways we die, simply ten ways listed on the most recent research conducted on mortality, based on 17,201 registered deaths caused by 'accidents and external causes' in 2011 in England and Wales. In all, there were 484,367 recorded deaths in 2011.

LIFE & DEATH

10 notable final words

1 **'Die, my dear? Why, that's the last thing I'll do!'** – The most commonly reported final words of Julius Henry 'Groucho' Marx, who died in 1977.

2 **'Bugger Bognor'** – King George V, whose physician had suggested, in 1936, that he head to his seaside palace in Bognor Regis to relax.

3 **'Don't worry – it's not loaded, see?'** – Terry Kath, guitarist and founding member of rock band Chicago, who died from a self-inflicted gunshot wound in 1978.

4 **'Oh, wow. Oh, wow. Oh, wow.'** – Apple co-founder Steve Jobs on his deathbed in 2011, with his eyes fixed on the middle distance.

5 **'I know you are here to kill me. Shoot, coward, you are only going to kill a man.'** – Ernesto 'Che' Guevara, Cuban revolutionary, addressing his firing squad in Bolivia in 1967.

6 **'I'm bored with it all.'** – Winston Churchill, prior to a severe stroke that took his life, aged 90, in 1965.

7 **'Stopped.'** – Celebrated English surgeon Joseph Henry Green, having checked his own pulse in 1863.

8 **'Either that wallpaper goes, or I do.'** – The widely reported last words of Oscar Wilde, spoken before dying of cerebral meningitis in 1900.

9 **'I'd like to have some milk. Please, please give me some more.'** – Pop prince Michael Jackson in 2009. The 'milk' was an IV drip of the anaesthetic Propfol (Diprivan) administered by his doctor Conrad Murray, along with a cocktail of drugs, prior to Jackson's cardiac arrest. Murray was later jailed for involuntary manslaughter

10 **'I told you I was ill.'** – The words carved into Spike Milligan's gravestone. He died in 2002.

Top 10 TV theme tunes played at funerals

- *Match of the Day*

- *Pot Black*

- *One Foot in the Grave*

- *Last of the Summer Wine*

- *Dr Who*

- *The X Files*

- *Red Dwarf*

- *Top Gear*

- *Six Feet Under*

- '*The Muppets* Theme Tune' ('It's Time to Play the Music')

Source: The Co-operative Funeralcare, 2012, www.co-operative.coop

10 ridiculously expensive hamburgers

BURGER	RESTAURANT/LOCATION	PRICE

1 Fleur Burger 5000 — Fleur (Las Vegas, Nevada, USA) — $5,000 (£3,084)

Wagyu beef, foie gras, truffle, on a brioche bun, served with a bottle of 1995 Château Petrus.

2 777 Burger — Le Burger Brassiere (Las Vegas, Nevada, USA) — $777 (£480)

Kobe beef, Maine lobster, 100-year-aged balsamic vinegar, served with a bottle of Dom Pérignon.

3 The Douche Burger‡ — 666 Burger (New York, USA) — $666 (£410)

Kobe beef, lobster, truffle, caviar, foie gras, served in a gold leaf wrapper.

4 Le Burger Extravagant — Serendipity 3 (New York, USA) — $295 (£182)

Wagyu beef, black truffle, caviar, quail egg, presented with a diamond-encrusted gold toothpick.

5 The Burger§ — Burger King (London) — $190 (£95)

Wagyu beef, truffle, Pata Negra prosciutto, on an Iranian saffron and truffle bun.

6 The X Burger — W Hotel (Seoul, South Korea) — $160 (£98)

Australian Wagyu beef, foie gras, black truffle, lobster tail, truffle aioli, on a brioche bun.

BURGER	RESTAURANT/LOCATION	PRICE*

DB Royale Double Truffle Burger — DB Bistro Moderne (New York)/ Daniel Boulud Brasserie (Las Vegas, Nevada, USA) — $140 (£86)

Sirloin braised short ribs, foie gras, black truffle, on a Parmesan bun.

Million Rupiah Hamburger — Four Seasons Hotel (Jakarta, Indonesia) — $108 (£68)

Japanese Kobe beef, foie gras, wasabi mayonnaise, portobello mushrooms and Korean pears.

The Tri-Burger — Old Homestead Steakhouse (Boca Raton, Florida, USA) — $100 (£61)

USDA Prime, Japanese Wagyu and Argentinean beef.

The Rossini — Burger Bar (Las Vegas, Nevada, USA) — $60 (£37)

Australian Wagyu beef, foie gras, shaved truffle, black Perigord truffle sauce.

*Prices correct at time of availability (not every burger is still on sale); all prices given in US$ for comparison and converted into pounds sterling November 2013

†$70 (£43) for burger only

‡Despite widespread publicity, the Douche Burger turned out to be a hoax. 'Created' by a New York food cart, it was an ode to excess created to lampoon the fashion for obnoxiously expensive hamburgers. But it was never cooked or sold

§Sold for a limited time only and for charity

10 famous foods named after real people

1 **Eggs Benedict** – Supposedly the request of a hung-over Lemuel Benedict one morning in 1894; he requested a dish of English muffins topped with ham, poached eggs and Hollandaise sauce.

2 **Granny Smith apples** – Named after the British–Australian granny Marie Ana Smith, the orchardist responsible for the cultivation of the apple in 1868.

3 **Caesar Salad** – Reportedly named after the chef Caesar Cardini, who threw the dish together using what he had left at the Hotel Caesar in Tijuana, Mexico, in 1924.

4 **Pavlova** – Named after Russian ballerina Anna Pavlova (1881–1931), the meringue celebrated as being as 'light as Pavlova'. The creation was born in either Australia or New Zealand, depending on who you believe.

5 **Nachos** – Reputedly the creation of Ignacio 'Nacho' Anaya, maître d' at the Victory Club in Piedras Negras, Mexico, who added cheese and jalapeños to fried corn tortillas in 1943. They went on the menu as 'Nachos Especiales'.

6 **Beef Wellington** – Created to honour the 1st Duke of Wellington, either to honour his heroics in the Battle of Waterloo, or as a patriotic rebranding of France's similar filet de boeuf en croûte.

7 **Stroganov** – Classic Russian beef dish, most likely named after the influential Russian Stroganov family.

8 **Battenberg cake** – Marzipan-heavy 'window' cake, most likely named after late 19th-century aristocratic Battenberg family, who changed their name to Mountbatten during the First World War.

9 **Pizza Margherita** – Cheese, tomato and basil pizza, named after Queen Margherita of Savoy, who chose it on a trip to Naples around 1889.

10 **Garibaldi biscuits** – Named after Italian general and politician Giuseppe Garibaldi, following a visit to England in 1864.

Top 10 most popular McDonald's menu items*

- Fries

- Coca-Cola

- Big Mac®

- Double Cheeseburger

- Cheeseburger

- Hash Brown

- Chicken McNuggets® Happy Meal

- Quarter Pounder with Cheese

- Diet Coke

- Strawberry Milkshake

*August 2008–July 2013, UK sales only
Source: McDonald's

Top 10 curries in Britain*

1 Chicken tikka masala

2 Chicken jalfrezi

3 Chicken korma

4 Meat madras

5 Lamb rogan josh

6 Chicken dhansak

7 Lamb bhuna

8 Butter chicken

9 Balti (chicken, beef, prawn, lamb, vegetable)

10 Prawn korma

*As at 2012 and based on more than 4,000 votes

Source: National Curry Week, www.nationaleatingoutweek.com

Top 10 most popular sandwich ingredients*

INGREDIENT	ESTIMATED YEARLY CONSUMPTION
Bread (obviously)	252,000 tonnes
Chicken	55,600 tonnes
Cheese	19,900 tonnes
Egg	13,900 tonnes
Ham	12,600 tonnes
Prawn	7,600 tonnes
Bacon	6,300 tonnes
Tuna	5,700 tonnes
Salmon	3,800 tonnes
Beef	2,500 tonnes

*Based on the estimated amount of key ingredients used by the commercial sandwich market in 2012

Source: The British Sandwich Association, www.sandwich.org.uk

FYI: be aware that while chicken remains top of the proper list (discounting bread, for that's a given), the chook is gradually losing its dominance, with both egg and ham sandwiches gaining in popularity in recent years. They still have some ground to make up though and the chicken should remain out in front for the foreseeable future.

Top 10 most popular Walkers crisp flavours*

1. Cheese & Onion
2. Ready Salted
3. Salt & Vinegar
4. Prawn Cocktail
5. Smoky Bacon
6. Roast Chicken
7. Worcester Sauce
8. Tomato Ketchup
9. Pickled Onion
10. Sour Cream & Chive

*Based on figures for August 2012–August 2013

Source: www.pepsico.co.uk (owners of Walkers crisps)

O superfoods that will*
mprove your life

Red grapefruit - Eating one a day will lower LDL (bad) cholesterol by 20 per cent.

Broccoli - Contains vitamin K, which regulates insulin, so you have less chance of developing diabetes or being obese.

Cranberry juice - Three glasses a day will lower your risk of heart disease by 40 per cent.

Avocados - A source of potassium, which (combined with a low sodium diet) guards against high blood pressure and stroke.

Brown rice - Lowers your risk of diabetes, due to its vitamin B1.

Black turtle beans - Their antioxidants fend off disease. Costa Rica's Chorotega tribe eat them and have the most centenarians on earth.

Watercress - Increases levels of cancer-fighting antioxidants lutein and beta-carotene - 85 g (3 oz) a day gives maximum benefits.

Coffee - Four cups a day reduce your risk of dying of heart disease by 53 per cent.

Eggs - Carotenoids (lutein and zeaxanthin) help protect eyesight; sulphur and vitamin B12 improve the condition of your hair and skin.

Blueberries - The most super of the superfoods, antioxidants and flavonoids boost brain power and help fight against Alzheimer's, the dietary fibre and resveratrol reduce bad cholesterol, while the polyphenols, anthocyanins and collagen make you look younger.

*Might. No cast-iron promises

Source: *Men's Health*, www.menshealth.co.uk

10 dishes you might think twice about ordering overseas

1 **Holodets** (Russia/Ukraine) – Essentially meat set in jelly made by cooking pork parts that contain large amounts of skin, bone and cartilage, usually from the legs and hooves. Mixed with vegetables and spices, it's set in delicious aspic and chilled before serving.

2 **Cuy** (Peru) – Read the small print. Cuy is guinea pig, which in Peru is often roasted and served with potatoes or rice and a nice spicy sauce.

3 **Mopane Worm** (South Africa/Zimbabwe/Botswana) – A juicy caterpillar, cooked in a stew of tomatoes and onions. In some regions its guts are squeezed out first and the worm is fried in its own body fat. Sometimes served with pap, a maize porridge.

4 **Pekasam Ikan** (Malaysia) – How to make fermented fish taste a little more palatable? Coat it in yeast of course. That makes it far less rancid and transforms it into a national speciality.

5 **Czernina** (Poland) – Duck or goose blood soup, devised as a way to use up every last part of the poor bird. Typically cooked with dried fruits and vinegar, which is said to prevent the blood from clotting.

6 **Laab Luead** (Thailand) – A dish of delicious sour and spicy pork, but with a twist. The pork is raw and dressed with a generous splash of the pig's blood. Oink oink.

7 **Balut** (Philippines) – A developing duck embryo boiled alive and eaten in the shell. Popular street food in the Philippines and also common in Laos, Cambodia and Vietnam.

8 **Roast Sheep's Eyeballs** (Saudi Arabia) – A little like chomping into an oyster; a lot like being a contestant on *I'm a Celebrity*.

9 **Patsa** (Greece) – Just one variation on a dish very popular across Eastern Europe, but less so everywhere else. And who doesn't love a soup made of pigs' feet and stomach lining? Maybe order the pasta instead.

10 **Bosintang** (Korea) – A soup of mainly dog meat, with vegetables, spices and a medicinal plant named *Agastache rugosa* thrown in to hide the taste. What, you thought the dog business was just a myth?

10 apparently delicious insects and spiders

1 Red tree ants – Popular in Cambodia, this sour-tasting alternative to giant spiders is often included as an ingredient in stir-fries.

2 Ecsamoles – The eggs of the giant black *Liometopum* ant, they have a slightly nutty flavour and taste far less heinous than they should. Popular in Mexico, shoved between tacos.

3 Bamboo worm – Significantly longer and chunkier than your usual worms, these are frequently served as a deep-fried snack and are popular in Thailand.

4 Mealworms – Baked or fried, and supposedly as beneficial as fish and meat in terms of their nutrients. Oddly, they appear to be increasingly popular in Holland.

5 Scorpion – Usually deep-fried to add some crunch to a largely tasteless street snack found on the streets of Beijing, among other places.

6 Digger wasps – In Japan, frequently found baked into rice crackers.

7 Cockroach – Another popular snack in Cambodia, the cockroach tastes like cashew nuts when roasted, and like a crunchy, greasy insect when deep-fried.

8 Locust – Supposedly comparable in taste to fried chicken, also popular for a high fibre count and very popular in Japan.

9 Silkworm – Peddled in small paper cups around South Korea, silkworm pupae are made slightly more palatable by being boiled.

10 Tarantula – Venomous spider, fried, served with salt and high in protein. Tastes nutty. Another one popular in Cambodia.

Top 10 restaurants in the world*

RESTAURANT	LOCATION	2012 RANKING
1 **El Celler De Can Roca**†	Girona, Spain	2
2 **Noma**	Copenhagen, Denmark	1
3 **Osteria Francescana**	Modena, Italy	5
4 **Mugaritz**	San Sebastián, Spain	3
5 **Eleven Madison Park**	New York, USA	10
6 **D.O.M.**	São Paulo, Brazil	4
7 **Dinner by Heston Blumenthal**	London, UK	9
8 **Arzak**	San Sebastián, Spain	8
9 **Steirereck**	Vienna, Austria	11
10 **Vendôme**	Bergisch Gladbach, Germany	23

*2013 ranking

†Sample dish: Iberian suckling pig and charcoal-grilled king prawn with ink rocks, fried legs, head juice and king prawn essence (part of the €130 tasting menu)

Source: *Restaurant* magazine, 'The World's 50 Best Restaurants', sponsored by S.Pellegrino and Acqua Panna, www.theworlds50best.com

10 fad diets

The Sleeping Beauty Diet – By being heavily sedated for several days, the premise here is if you're sleeping, you're not eating. Elvis was supposedly a fan.

Fletcherism – Created by 'The Great Masticator' Horace Fletcher in the early 1900s. Everything was chewed thoroughly before being spat out, with only the vital nutrients and none of the calories swallowed.

The Leek Diet – A weekend diet consisting of only leeks, cooked and in broth. The diuretic nature of the vegetable helps dieters shed excess water.

The Baby Food Diet – Disciples, many of whom reside in Hollywood, switch one or two 'proper'-sized meals a day for a baby-sized jar of purée.

Fruitarianism – A diet of nothing but fruit, which some believe formed the original diet of mankind. Following this has been shown to lead to vitamin deficiencies.

The Cotton Wool Diet – Favoured by supermodels and imbeciles, the cotton wool makes the dieter feel full without containing calories. Sadly, cotton is not digestible so this is ill-advised.

The Tapeworm Diet – Devised in the early 1900s, when pills containing tapeworm were consumed. The worms would then attach to the stomach lining and absorb food. Nowadays it's considered highly dangerous.

The Master Cleanse Diet – Followers take a laxative morning and night, then survive on a light liquid diet of water, lemon or lime juice, maple syrup and cayenne pepper.

The Freegan Diet – Disciples adopt a regular vegan diet, but then survive on discarded scraps in an attempt to reduce society's waste. The diet is supplemented with wild plants.

Breatharianism – To followers of this dangerous diet, food and water are unnecessary and they can survive on their own breath and positive thinking. In reality, this approach soon leads to death.

10 foods that might easily kill you

❶ Fugu – The Japanese word for blowfish, this is an expensive delicacy in Japan, where it's cost some diners their lives. If prepared incorrectly, its intestines, ovaries and liver can release a highly toxic and frequently fatal poison.

❷ Cassava plant – A staple crop in Africa, Asia and South America, the cassava plant is used to make tapioca, if prepared correctly. However, if prepared incorrectly, it can produce a hefty dose of cyanide.

❸ Monkey brain – A delicacy in certain parts of Asia, but alongside the obvious horror of eating a monkey's brain, you may also be put off by the threat of the Variant Creutzfeldt-Jakob disease, which can lurk inside a monkey's skull and lead to death.

❹ Sannakji choking octopi – The name betrays this one. The octopus is seasoned with oil and sesame seeds, then served, but its suction cups can choke diners to death if not chewed sufficiently. Hard to feel much sympathy though.

❺ Silver-stripe blaasop – An Indian Ocean delicacy, but also found on occasion in the Mediterranean, these fish present no problem unless you eat the liver, reproductive organs or skin, for they can cause breathing problems and fatal muscle paralysis.

❻ Castor beans – Castor oil, from the castor bean plant, is widely available and safe to consume, providing it's been safely prepared and the poison extracted. Each bean is loaded with ricin, a deadly poison that can, if consumed in significant doses, lead to death within 36–72 hours.

7 **Casu Marzu** – A rotting Italian cheese left out in the open to invite flies to lay their eggs inside. The maggots inside hatch and eat into the cheese and speed up the fermentation process. Banned on the grounds of it being as dangerous as it is disgusting, if consumed the maggots can cause serious vomiting and diarrhoea.

8 **Ackee fruit** – Popular in Jamaica, the ackee contains a large black seed, which contains the poison hypoglycin. If eaten, the seed can cause severe sickness and in extreme cases death.

9 **Hotdogs** – An underestimated killer. Let's ignore the supposed risk of cancer from whatever it is they put in them and instead focus on the very real death-by-asphyxiation threat they present. A significant cause of food-related choking deaths each year, and while most victims are children, wieners don't discriminate.

10 **Giant bullfrog** – A speciality in Namibia. Most bullfrogs are safe to eat, should you be that way inclined. The danger comes from young bullfrogs, which still carry a poison within them that can cause temporary kidney failure. If you must eat him, ask him how old he is first.

10 last meals of the rich and famous

1 **Elvis Presley** – For his final breakfast, 'The King' had four scoops of ice cream and six chocolate chip cookies, then had a heart attack on the toilet. The diet and the departure may have been connected.

2 **Michael Jackson** – The King of Pop's last meal was reportedly seared ahi tuna with an organic salad and a glass of carrot and orange juice. He later died following a cardiac arrest.

3 **John Lennon** – Hours before being shot dead by a deranged fan in New York, Lennon ate a corned beef sandwich. A poor choice for a final meal, but then Lennon wasn't to know.

4 **Marilyn Monroe** – Hours after consuming a Mexican meal with Dom Pérignon champagne at a restaurant in Hollywood, Norma Jean either took her own life or was murdered, depending on which theory you believe.

5 **John F. Kennedy** – On the morning he was shot dead, the President took breakfast in his hotel room in Fort Worth, Texas. He reportedly ate two soft-boiled eggs, bacon, toast and marmalade, and drinking coffee and orange juice.

6 **Frank Sinatra** – Ol' Blue Eyes' last meal was a simple grilled cheese sandwich, which was half-eaten. He died following a heart attack.

7 **Jimi Hendrix** – The legendary fret-spanker's final meal was a tuna fish sandwich. He later died after choking on his own vomit – his death caused by asphyxia while intoxicated with barbiturates.

8 **Adolf Hitler** – Holed up in his bunker in Berlin with his new bride, Eva Braun, the moustachioed mad man reportedly dined on spaghetti with an unspecified 'light sauce', or lasagne, or vegetable soup and mashed potato – reports vary. Afterwards, they killed themselves.

9 **Liberace** – Before he died of an AIDS-related illness, the flamboyant showman's final meal was a disappointingly mundane, porridge-like Cream of Wheat hot cereal, made with semi-skimmed milk and sweetened with brown sugar.

10 **Princess Diana** – In the hours before her death, the Princess dined with her boyfriend, Dodi Al Fayed at L'Espadon restaurant in the Ritz. The Queen of our Hearts ate a delicate mushroom and asparagus omelette, Dover sole and vegetable tempura.

10 'final meal' requests*

1 **Cheez Doodles (crisps) and a can of Coca-Cola** – Requested by Velma Barfield, November 1984

2 **Two slices of cheese pizza, two cups of coffee** – Requested by Gary Heidnik, July 1999

3 **Two pints of mint chocolate chip ice cream** – Requested by Timothy McVeigh, June 2001

4 **Bacon and eggs** – Requested by Charles Peace, February 1879

5 **One lobster tail, fried potatoes, fried shrimp, 170 g (6 oz) fried clams, half a loaf of garlic bread and 950 ml (32 fl oz) of root beer** – Requested by Allen Lee 'Tiny' Davis, July 1999

6 **Twelve fried shrimp, a bucket of original recipe KFC, French fries and 450 g (1 lb) of strawberries** – Requested by John Wayne Gacy, May 1994.

7 **One large vegetarian pizza, to be given to a homeless person in Nashville, Tennessee** – Requested by Philip Workman, May 2007†

8 **One cup of coffee** – Requested by Aileen Wuornos, October 2002

9 **One 340 g (12 oz) box of assorted chocolates and 1 litre (2 pints) of German chocolate ice cream** – Requested by William Happ, October 2013

10 **A single olive –** Requested by Victor Feguer, March 1963

*Of condemned criminals on Death Row in the USA

†Although this was denied, local homeless shelters received several hundred pizzas donated by residents who had heard about Philip Workman's request

10 national food and drink days in the USA

FOOD & DRINK

NATIONAL DAY	DATE
1 National Cream Puff Day	2 January
2 National Something on a Stick Day	8 March
3 National Turkey Neck Soup Day	30 March
4 National Pigs-in-a-Blanket Day	24 April
5 National German Chocolate Cake Day	11 June
6 National Jerky Day	12 June
7 National Drink Beer Day	28 September
8 National Yorkshire Pudding Day	13 October
9 National Gummy Worm Day	15 July
10 National Pizza With Everything (Except Anchovies) Day	12 November

*Every day of the year in the USA has been designated a day of gastronomic celebration.

10 Second World War basic weekly food rations

FOOD ITEM	AMOUNT*
1 **Meat**	2 small chops
2 **Bacon and ham**	113 g (4 oz)
3 **Butter**	113 g (4 oz)
4 **Cheese**	56 g (2 oz)
5 **Margarine**	113 g (4 oz)
6 **Cooking fat**	113 g (4 oz)
7 **Milk**	1.7 litres (3 pints)†
8 **Sugar**	226 g (8 oz)
9 **Tea**	56 g (2 oz)
10 **Eggs**	1‡

*Quantities fluctuated throughout the Second World War but these figures represent rationing for one adult – children received half as much

†Plus 1 packet of dried milk per month

‡Plus 1 packet of dried egg per month

Source: Imperial War Museum, www.iwm.org.uk

This list was supplemented by a monthly points system to enable additional purchases, such as canned fruit, breakfast cereals and biscuits.

10 courses served aboard RMS *Titanic*

FOOD & DRINK

1 **First Course** – Hors D'Oeuvres; Oysters

2 **Second Course** – Consommé Olga; Cream of Barley Soup

3 **Third Course** – Poached Salmon with Mousseline Sauce, Cucumbers

4 **Fourth Course** – Filet Mignons Lili; Sauté of Chicken, Lyonnaise; Vegetable Marrow Farci

5 **Fifth Course** – Lamb, Mint Sauce; Roast Duckling, Apple Sauce; Sirloin of Beef, Chateau Potatoes; Green Peas; Creamed Carrots; Boiled Rice; Parmentier and Boiled Potatoes

6 **Sixth Course –** Punch Romaine

7 **Seventh Course** – Roast Squab and Cress

8 **Eighth Course** – Cold Asparagus Vinaigrette

9 **Ninth Course** – Pâté de Foie Gras; Celery

10 **Tenth Course** – Waldorf Pudding; Peaches in Chartreuse Jelly; Chocolate and Vanilla Éclairs; French Ice Cream

Source: Rick Archbold and Dana McCauley, *Last Dinner on the Titanic* (Madison Press Books, 1997)

Oblivious to the iceberg up ahead, on the evening of 14 April 1912, the first-class passengers aboard the *Titanic* enjoyed this gut-busting 10-course banquet. Each course was paired with fine wines and, upon completion, guests were offered spirits and cigars.

10 extremely strong bottles of booze

DRINK	COUNTRY OF ORIGIN	PROOF (USA)	ALCOHOL BY VOLUME (UK)
1 Spirytus Delikatesowy Vodka	Poland	192	96%
2 Everclear (Grain Alcohol)	USA	190	95%
3 Bruichladdich X4 Quadrupled Whisky	Scotland	184	92%
4 River Antoine Royale Grenadian Rum	Grenada	180	90%
5 Hapsburg Gold Label Premium Reserve Absinthe	Czech Republic	179	89.9%
5 Pincer Vodka – Shanghai Strength	Scotland	177	88.8%
7 New Jersey Devil Springs Vodka	USA	160	80%
7 John Crow Batty Rum	Jamaica	160	80%
9 Inner Circle Black Rum	Australia	151	75.9%
10 Bacardi 151 (rum)	Puerto Rico	151	75.5%

'Proof' and 'percentage' are the two most recognized ways of measuring a drink's alcohol (ethanol) content. The UK uses percentage (ABV, 'alcohol by volume'); the US uses 'proof' (which is twice the alcohol content, so 160 proof equals 80 per cent alcohol content). Many of these drinks are created as the base of drinks, rather than to be drunk neat. Always read the label and, of course, always drink responsibly.

Top 10 strongest beers*

1 **Snake Venom: 67% ABV** – Brewed in Scotland by Brewmeister.

2 **Armageddon: 65% ABV** – Brewed in Scotland by Brewmeister.

3 **Start the Future: 60% ABV** – Brewed in Holland by 't Koelschip.

4 **Schorschbock 57% Finis Coronat Opus: 57% ABV** – Brewed in Germany by Schorschbräu.

5 **End of History: 55% ABV** – Brewed in Scotland by BrewDog.

6 **Schorschbräu 43: 43% ABV** – Brewed in Germany by Schorschbräu

7 **Sink the Bismarck: 41% ABV** – Brewed in Scotland by BrewDog.

8 **Esprit de Nöel: 40% ABV** – Brewed in Italy by Baladin.

9 **Black Damnation VI: 39% ABV** – Brewed in Belgium by De Struise Brouwers.

10 **Cat Freeze The Penguin: 35% ABV** – Brewed in Italy by The Revelation Cat Craft brewery.

*November 2013 ranking

Source: *The Drinks Business*, www.thedrinksbusiness.com

Many of the beers on this list were brewed from 2010 on, when BrewDog and Schorschbräu battled it out to produce the world's strongest beer. Given their vicious strength, these beers are designed to be sipped like a spirit rather than guzzled like a pint.

10 sizes of champagne bottle

SIZE	BOTTLE CAPACITY	VOLUME
1 **Piccolo**	Quarter-bottle	0.2 litre (0.35 pint)
2 **Demi**	Half-bottle	0.375 litre (0.66 pint)
3 **Magnum**	2 bottles	1.5 litres (2.6 pints)
4 **Jeroboam**	4 bottles	3 litres (5.2 pints)
5 **Rehoboam**	6 bottles	4.5 litres (7.9 pints)
6 **Methuselah**	8 bottles	6 litres (10.5 pints)
7 **Salmanazar**	12 bottles	9 litres (15.8 pints)
8 **Balthazar**	16 bottles	12 litres (21.1 pints)
9 **Nebuchadnezzar**	20 bottles	15 litres (26.4 pints)
10 **Melchior**	24 bottles	18 litres (31.7 pints)

A standard champagne bottle contains 0.75 litres (1.3 pints).

10 unconventional hangover cures

1 **A Prairie Oyster** – A raw egg mixed with lemon juice or vinegar, pepper and Worcestershire sauce. The yolk should be left intact and the heinous concoction swallowed in one.

2 **A Suffering Bastard** – Concocted in a Cairo hotel and mixing equal measures of brandy, gin and lime juice and a splash of Angostura bitters. Stir, drink, feel drunk again but now less hung over.

3 **Rassol** – A vegetable brine with various herbs and spices, plus finely cut lamb if really pushing the boat out. Rassol is popular in Russia, a nation which suffers more hangovers than most.

4 **Lemons and limes** – Half a lemon or lime, with the juicy part rubbed around the sufferer's armpits – some claim you only need to grease the pit of your drinking arm, but it can't hurt to do both. Puerto Ricans swear by it.

5 **Bull penis** – No longer attached to the bull, and always dried. Supposedly once favoured by hung-over Sicilians, to shake the fug and restore vitality. At a guess, a stick of Peperami might work just as well.

6 **Jeeves' secret concoction** – To revive the imbecilic Wooster from his booze-induced misery, his ever-patient butler Jeeves mixed cognac, tomato juice and raw egg, then served it in a crystal glass on a silver tray.

Pickled herring – A herring fillet wrapped around small chunks of onion, cucumber or gherkin. Eat until you feel less nauseous or are sick, which will make you feel better in the long run. Popular in Germany.

Deep-fried canaries – The Ancient Romans eased their pounding heads by deep-frying a canary in oil and seasoning it with salt and pepper. One probably best avoided.

Sheep lungs and owl eggs – The Ancient Greeks supposedly chased away their hangovers by feasting on a hearty repast of sheep lungs and two owl eggs. Poached, boiled or scrambled, the choice is yours.

Bottle cork – In Haiti, where voodoo still rules, if they have no sheep lungs, some claim that by sticking 13 black-headed pins into the cork of the bottle that caused the pain, the hangover will magically lift.

Top 10 most common cars on the roads in Britain

MODEL	NUMBER OF CARS
1 **Ford Focus**	1,438,778
2 **Ford Fiesta**	1,317,119
3 **Vauxhall Corsa**	1,151,586
4 **Vauxhall Astra**	1,106,383
5 **Volkswagen Golf**	943,566
6 **BMW 3 Series**	643,403
7 **Renault Clio**	632,572
8 **Volkswagen Polo**	575,545
9 **Ford Mondeo**	542,288
10 **Peugeot 206**	500,950

*Registered up to end March 2013

Source: The Department of Transport, www.gov.uk

If you suspected that you can't drive more than a few yards without encountering a traffic jam, you are right and it's with good reason: according to 2013 figures, there are approximately 34.5 million vehicles clogging up the roads of Great Britain. Some 28.7 million of them are cars (up 35 per cent, from 21.2 million in 1994).

The 10 most dangerous roads in the UK*

SECTION OF ROAD	LOCATION	DISTANCE
1 A537 Macclesfield to Buxton	Cheshire/Derbyshire	12 km (7.5 miles)
2 A5012 Pikehall to Matlock	Derbyshire	15 km (9.3 miles)
3 A621 Baslow to Totley	Derbyshire/ South Yorkshire	9 km (5.6 miles)
4 A625 Calver to Sheffield	South Yorkshire	13 km (8 miles)
5 A54 Congleton to Buxton	Derbyshire	24 km (14.9 miles)
6 A581 Rufford to Chorley	Lancashire	11 km (6.8 miles)
7 A5004 Whaley Bridge to Buxton	Derbyshire	12 km (7.5 miles)
8 A675 Blackburn to Preston	Lancashire	7 km (4.3 miles)
9 A61 Barnsley to Wakefield	Yorkshire	10 km (6.2 miles)
10 A285 Chichester to Petworth	West Sussex	19 km (11.8 miles)

*According to a Road Safety Foundation report covering 45,000 km (28,000 miles) of A-roads and motorways in the UK, based on the number of crashes (serious and fatal) on sections of road between 2007 and 2011

Source: Road Safety Foundation, 'Saving Lives for Less', October 2013

10 implausible but genuine motor insurance claims

1 'The guy was all over the road. I had to swerve a number of times before I hit him.'

2 'I started to slow down but the traffic was more stationary than I thought.'

3 'The gentleman behind me struck me on the backside. He then went to rest in a bush with just his rear end showing.'

4 'Coming home I drove into the wrong house and collided with a tree I don't have.'

5 'I told the police that I was not injured, but on removing my hat found that I had a fractured skull.'

6 'I pulled away from the side of the road, glanced at my mother-in-law and headed over the embankment.'

7 'I didn't think the speed limit applied after midnight.'

8 'I had been driving for 40 years when I fell asleep at the wheel and had an accident.'

9 'I left for work this morning at 7 a.m. as usual when I collided straight into a bus. The bus was five minutes early.'

10 'I pulled in to the side of the road because there was smoke coming from under the hood. I realized there was a fire in the engine, so I took my dog and smothered it with a blanket.'

Source: Businessballs.com

0 excellent car facts*

The first recorded automobile accident occurred in 1769 – The car is still preserved in the Conservatoire Nationale des Artiers in Paris.

Stockcar racing has its origins in moonshine runners – To transport illicitly distilled or smuggled alcohol, bootleggers modified their cars so that they could outrun police cars in prohibition-era America.

The iconic Rolls-Royce hood ornament is called the Spirit of Ecstasy – In 2008, a special diamond-encrusted version was designed with an asking price of $200,000.

£30 – That's the cost of using a car horn while stationary in the UK.

$1,000,000 – The largest speeding fine ever, given to a Swedish man who was clocked doing 290 km/h (180 mph) in Switzerland, where fines are proportionate to income.

Volkswagen allegedly named many of its cars after ocean currents and winds – Passat (after the German word for trade wind), Polo (after polar winds), Golf (after Gulf Stream), and Jetta (after jet stream).

On average, British drivers will be stuck in traffic jams nearly 10,000 times, spending the equivalent of 99 days of their life going nowhere.

Many British traffic police carry teddy bears in their vehicles – They use them to console children after car crashes.

Six months – The time it would take to reach the moon if you could drive straight upwards at 97 km/h (60 mph).

256 – The number of times you can press an out-of-range car remote key before it will stop working. This is due to the method of encryption between the car remote and the receiver in the vehicle.

*Correct as at December 2013
Source: www.carloan4u.co.uk

10 of the fastest cars on the planet*

CAR	TOP SPEED
1 **Koenigsegg Agera R**	439.3 km/h (273 mph)
2 **Bugatti Veyron Super Sport**	430.9 km/h (267.8 mph)
3 **Hennessey Venom GT**	427.6 km/h (265.7 mph)
4 **9ff GT9-R**	413.6 km/h (257 mph)
5 **SSC Ultimate Aero**	412.28 km/h (256.18 mph)
6 **Bugatti Veyron Grand Sport Vitesse**	408.8 km/h (254.04 mph)
7 **Saleen S7 Twin-Turbo**	399.1 km/h (248 mph)
8 **Koenigsegg CCX**	394.3 km/h (245 mph)
9 **McLaren F1**	391 km/h (243 mph)
10 **Zenvo ST1**	374.9 km/h (233 mph)

*Based on speed (uncertified) rather than acceleration; ranking correct as at May 2013

†This list cannot claim to be the definitive 10 fastest cars on the planet because not all the above speeds have been certified. If we were to go on certification alone, the Bugatti Veyron Super Sport would be the fastest car in the world. For the full list of all contenders, see www.autosaur.com

Source: Autosaur, www.autosaur.com

Top 10 most stolen cars in the UK*

MAKE/MODEL	NUMBER STOLEN†
Mitsubishi Pajero	647
Nissan Sunny	332
Nissan Bluebird	316
BMW X6	183
Ford Orion	176
Rover Metro	116
Vauxhall Nova	98
Vauxhall Cavalier	95
Toyota Previa	86
Ford Granada	83

*According to the Car Crime Census 2013 compiled by www.honestjohn.co.uk; based on figures for the period October 2011 to September 2012

†Per 10,000 vehicles registered. Cars with less than 1,000 registered in the UK have been omitted. For reference, the average theft rate is 28 per 10,000

Source: www.honestjohn.co.uk

Many of the cars on the list rank highly because they are easy to target thanks to a lack of security or are in high demand as 'steal-to-order' cars.

The 10 worst maritime disasters*

SHIP/INCIDENT/YEAR	ESTIMATED NUMBER KILLED

1 **MV *Doña Paz*: 1987**   4,04
This Philippine-registered passenger ferry collided with oil tanker
MT *Vector* in the Tablas Strait, near Marinduque.

2 ***Kiangya*: 1948**   2,750–3,920
Passenger steamship that blew up and sank in the mouth of the
Huangpu River, 80 km (50 miles) south of Shanghai, reportedly
hitting a mine left during the Second World War.

3 ***Mont-Blanc*: 1917**   2,000
This French cargo ship loaded with wartime explosives collided
with Norwegian ship *Imo* in Halifax Harbour, Nova Scotia. The result
were predictably tragic.

4 ***Le Joola*: 2002**   1,800+
A dangerously overloaded Senegalese state-run ferry, *Le Joola*
capsized in rough seas off the coast of Gambia.

5 ***Tek Sing*: 1822**   1,600
Labelled the '*Titanic* of the East', this Chinese sailing vessel was
packed full of passengers and porcelain when it ran aground on
a reef near Indonesia, sending hundreds to their deaths.

6 **SS *Sultana*: 1865**   1,54
An overloaded US steamboat heading down the Mississippi River,
the *Sultana* reached as far as Memphis, Tennessee, when three
of its boilers exploded and caused carnage.

SHIP/INCIDENT/DATE	ESTIMATED NUMBER KILLED

RMS *Titanic*: 1912 — 1,517
Celebrated passenger liner and world's largest ship, the *Titanic* famously struck an iceberg on its maiden voyage. Only 706 of the 2,223 on board survived to tell the tragic tale.

The Scilly naval disaster: 1707 — 1,400–2,000
On the night of 22 October, a Royal Navy fleet – HMS *Association*, HMS *Eagle*, HMS *Romney* and HMS *Firebrand* – all sank, unable to navigate through reefs to the west of the Isles of Scilly.

Toya Maru: 1954 — 1,153
This Japanese passenger ferry sank in the Tsugaru Strait between the islands of Hokkaido and Honshu; more than a thousand passengers were swept to their deaths by Typhoon Marie.

General Slocum paddle steamer: 1891 — 1,021
Packed with 1,300 passengers and travelling along New York's East River, the *General Slocum* caught fire early in its journey; most on board drowned or were burned alive.

*Not including vessels sunk during conflicts. The nature of many maritime disasters – overcrowded vessels with ticketless passengers – makes it hard to put an exact figure on fatalities. Figures are the most accurate available

For the record, including wartime disasters, the sinking of the MV *Wilhelm Gustoff* in January 1945 is currently the deadliest maritime disaster in history. Torpedoed and sunk by Soviet subs, the German ship sank inside 70 minutes, claiming the lives of 9,343 passengers, most of them refugees.

Top 10 busiest airports in the world*

AIRPORT	LOCATION	TOTAL NUMBER OF PASSENGERS
① Atlanta (ATL)	USA	94,615,321
② Beijing (PEK)	China	83,297,339
③ London (LHR)	UK	71,903,158
④ Tokyo (HND)	Japan	68,772,92?
⑤ Chicago (ORD)	USA	66,151,348
⑥ Los Angeles (LAX)	USA	65,797,737
⑦ Dubai (DXB)	United Arab Emirates	64,498,37?
⑧ Paris (CDG)	France	61,719,240
⑨ Dallas/Fort Worth (DFW)	USA	60,282,98?
⑩ Jakarta (CGK)	Indonesia	59,423,57?

*Based on airports participating in the ACI Monthly Traffic Statistics Collection

†Passenger traffic totals for the 12-month period ending 2013 – the results cover passengers enplaned and deplaned; passengers in transit counted once.

Source: Airports Council International

0 great sporting nicknames

'Whispering Death' – The terrifyingly rapid West Indies fast bowler Michael Holding, who took 249 Test wickets using a technique that was quiet but deadly. The finest nickname in sport was bestowed upon him by the admiring umpire Dicky Bird.

Neil 'Dissa' Pointon – Sometime nickname of the steady if unspectacular Manchester City, Everton and Oldham defender. Say it again, slowly.

'The Turbanator' – The possibly-now-frowned-upon-in-these-more-enlightened-times nickname of the turban-topped Indian spinner, cricketer Harbhajan Singh.

'The King of Spain' – Ahead of his testimonial year for Warwickshire, Ashley Giles had mugs printed declaring the legend 'King of Spin'. A printing error added in a rogue 'a' and a new legend was born.

'One Size' Fitz Hall – The defender-midfielder who has turned out for Southampton, Crystal Palace, QPR, Watford and others, and who possibly boasts football's finest ever nickname.

'The Raging Potato' – Keith Wood, the rampaging Irish and Lions hooker with the bald, potato-shaped head, according to rugby fans.

'Suitcase' – Ice hockey veteran Mike 'Suitcase' Sillinger set a record (12) for the number of NHL teams he played for, very rarely making it through a full season without being traded and moving on.

Martin 'Chariots' Offiah – Fleet-footed rugby league and union star who represented England, Great Britain, Widnes, Wigan and London Wasps. The name supposedly originated in the *Daily Star*.

'Mrs. Doubtfire' – Obvious but too good to deny entry here, the nickname beloved of American galleries to guarantee hot plumes of angry smoke billowed from both ears of golfer Colin Montgomerie. Inspired by the lead character in the film of the same name, played by an in-drag Robin Williams.

'The Round Mound of Rebound' – Also answering to 'Chuck' and 'Sir Charles', NBA All-Star Charles Barkley was nicknamed this thanks to his odd build and his remarkable ability to win rebounds.

Top 10 toughest endurance races on the planet*

RACE/LOCATION	DISTANCE/DURATION	TOTAL ASCENT	AVERAGE COMPLETION RATE
1 **Spartathlon** (Greece)	246 km (152 miles) in 36 hours	2,000 m (6,562 ft)	40
2 **Copper Canyon Ultra Marathon** (Mexico)	80 km (50 miles) in daylight hours	3,000 m (9,842 ft)	50
3 **Ultra Trail Mont Blanc** (France)	166 km (103 miles) in 46 hours	9,600 m (31,500 ft)	60
4 **Atacama Crossing** (Chile)	250 km (155 miles), daily stages	4,000 m (13,125 ft)	78
5 **Badwater Ultramarathon** (USA)	217 km (135 miles) in 48 hours	3,962 m (13,000 ft)	90
6 **Isle of Jura Fell Race** (UK)	28 km (17 miles) in daylight hours	2,370 m (7,776 ft)	94
=7 **Marathon des Sables** (Morocco)	242 km (150 miles) in 7 days	Varies annually	95
=7 **Everest Marathon** (Nepal)	42 km (26.2 miles) in daylight hours	700 m (2,300 ft)	95
9 **Snowdonia Marathon** (UK)	42 km (26.2 miles), 4-hour cut-off at 32 km (20 miles)	771 m (2,530 ft)	97
10 **Cuban Trail Marathon** (Cuba)	42 km (26.2 miles), no time limit	about 2,400 m (7,900 ft)	100

*Ranked by the percentage of participants who manage to complete the race

Source: *Outdoor Fitness* magazine, September 2011, www.outdoorfitnessmag.com

Top 10 most popular sports teams

TEAM	FANS*
FC Barcelona	42,680,849
Real Madrid CF	38,391,783
Manchester United FC	33,696,211
Chelsea FC	17,205,888
Los Angeles Lakers	16,351,755
AC Milan	15,691,813
Arsenal FC	14,068,018
Liverpool FC	12,151,171
Ferrari (F1)	11,779,611
Chicago Bulls	8,682,474

*According to that modern barometer of global popularity: Facebook likes as at September 2013

Source: ZenithOptimedia and Sponsorship Intelligence, using research and analysis tool Socialtools to produce The Social League, which ranks sports teams around the world according to their popularity on social media

Top 10 nations at the Summer Olympics*

COUNTRY	TOTAL MEDALS	GOLD MEDA
1 USA	2,424	99⬤
2 USSR	1,010	39
3 Great Britain	811	24
4 France	727	22
5 Germany	728	21
6 Italy	577	2⬤
7 China	473	2C
8 Hungary	490	17⬤
9 Sweden	497	14⬤
10 Australia	475	13⬤

*Ranked by number of gold medals; up to and including London 2012

Source: International Olympic Committee, via www.sports-reference.com

Top 10 alternative nations at the Summer Olympics*

COUNTRY	MEDALS	POPULATION	POPULATION PER MEDAL
Finland	302 (101 gold)	5,407,040	17,904
Sweden	483 (143 gold)	9,490,683	19,649
Hungary	475 (167 gold)	9,962,000	20,972
Denmark	179 (43 gold)	5,580,516	31,176
Bahamas	11 (5 gold)	353,658	32,150
Norway	149 (56 gold)	5,005,700	33,595
Bulgaria	214 (51 gold)	7,364,570	34,413
East Germany	409 (153 gold)	16,111,000	39,391
Estonia	33 (9 gold)	1,318,005	39,939
Jamaica	67 (17 gold)	2,705,827	40,385

*Ranked by countries' population per medal; up to and including London 2012

Source: Medals per Capita: Olympic Glory in Proportion, www.medalspercapita.com

Top 10 nations at the Winter Olympics*

SPORT

COUNTRY	TOTAL MEDALS	GOLD MEDALS
1 Norway	303	10?
2 USA	254	8?
3 Germany	207	7?
4 USSR	194	7?
5 Austria	201	5?
6 Canada	145	5?
7 Sweden	129	4?
8 Switzerland	127	4?
9 Finland	156	4?
10 East Germany	110	39

*Ranked by number of gold medals; up to and including Vancouver 2010
Where gold medals are equal, nations are ranked by total medals

**Source: International Olympic Committee,
via www.sports-reference.com**

Top 10 greatest British Olympians

ATHLETE	EVENT	YEARS	MEDALS*
Chris Hoy	Cycling	2000–12	6 gold, 1 silver
Steve Redgrave	Rowing	1984–2000	5 gold, 1 bronze
Bradley Wiggins	Cycling	2000–2012	4 gold, 1 silver, 2 bronze
Ben Ainslie	Sailing	1996–2012	4 gold, 1 silver
Matthew Pinsent	Rowing	1992–2004	4 gold
Paulo Radmilovic	Swimming, water polo	1908–20	4 gold
Jack Beresford	Rowing	1920–36	3 gold, 2 silver
Jason Kenny	Cycling	2008–12	3 gold, 1 silver
Henry Taylor	Swimming	1908–20	3 gold, 2 bronze
Reginald Doherty	Tennis	1900–1908	3 gold, 1 bronze

*Up to and including London 2012

10 defunct Olympic sports

1 **Distance plunge** – Having dived into the pool, Olympians compete to see who could travel furthest underwater without moving their limbs. A real feast for spectators, it was first seen at the St. Louis 1904 Olympic Games, but has never resurfaced since.

2 **Real pigeon shooting** – Like clay pigeon shooting, only using real pigeons. More than 300 reportedly perished before the Olympic organizers had a rethink. Its only appearance came at the Paris Games in 1900.

3 **Tug-of-war** – More often seen on the village green, this simple rope pull somehow lasted as an Olympic discipline from Paris 1900 to Antwerp 1920. During which time, Great Britain yanked itself to two golds and a silver.

4 **Rope climb** – Competitors attempted to climb a length of rope suspended from the ceiling as quickly as possible. More surprising than the fact it lasted from 1896 until Los Angeles 1932 was the fact the gold at the 1904 Games was taken by a man with a wooden leg.

5 **Duelling pistols** – Sadly, far less engaging than it sounds, the event required competitors not to shoot at each other from ten paces but to take potshots at mannequins dressed in frock coats from 20 m (65 ft) and 30 m (100 ft). Its first appearance, in 1912, was also its last.

Obstacle race – A precursor to *It's A Knockout* in which competitors took on an obstacle course over 200 m (650 ft), going up poles and over and under a series of floating boats on the River Seine. Debuted and died at the somewhat experimental Paris 1900 Olympic Games.

Croquet – The back-garden pastime of the upper classes also made its debut at Paris 1900, and was marked down as having 'hardly any pretensions to athleticism'. It was reported that only one person paid to watch an event that has never since reappeared.

Roque – Like croquet, but an American version, introduced at the St. Louis 1904 Games. Proved to be no more successful than proper croquet before it and was dropped by the time London 1908 came around.

Horse long-jump – A test of how far a nag could leap, and the answer was 6.1 m (20 ft) – the winning jump of the horse Extra Dry and its rider Constant van Langendonck in its debut at the 1900 Games. Discontinued thereafter.

One-handed weightlifting – Thrice thrust into the Olympic spotlight, one-handed weightlifting demanded competitors had to lift with each hand, with the winner determined from the combined score of both hands. Debuted in 1896, defunct by 1906.

10 significant 100 metre record times

TIME (SECS)	ATHLETE	COUNTRY	DATE
① 9.58	Usain Bolt	Jamaica	Aug 2009
② 9.69	Usain Bolt	Jamaica	Aug 2008
③ 9.72	Usain Bolt	Jamaica	May 2008
④ 9.74	Asafa Powell	Jamaica	Sep 2007
⑤ 9.77	Asafa Powell	Jamaica	Jun 2005
⑥ 9.78	Tim Montgomery*	USA	Sept 2002
⑦ 9.86	Carl Lewis†	USA	Aug 1991
⑧ 9.95	Jim Hines‡	USA	Oct 1968
⑨ 10.2	Jesse Owens§	USA	Jun 1936
⑩ 10.6	Donald Lippincott¶	USA	Jul 1912

*Record rescinded following disqualification for banned drug use

†Record stood for three years

‡Record stood for 15 years

§Record stood for 20 years

¶The first 100 metre record holder; record stood for nine years

This is only a snapshot of some significant 100 metre record times, a race recognized for the first time in 1912 by the International Amateur Athletics Federation. In just over a decade, the 100 metre world record has been redefined 18 times. Between 1912 and December 2013, the record has been held by 14 men.

0 Olympic Games moments

Ben Johnson shocks the world in the 100 metre final, powered by drugs. (Seoul 1988)

Usain Bolt showboats his way to gold. (Beijing 2008)

Michael Johnson obliterates the 200 metre final field. (Atlanta 1996)

Steve Redgrave rows his way to gold medals at five consecutive Olympic Games. (Sydney 2000)

Bob Beamon long-jumps 8.9 m (29 ft 2.5 in) into history. (Mexico City 1968)

The Munich massacre. Eleven athletes are taken hostage and killed by terrorists. (Munich 1972)

Jesse Owens takes gold before a seething Adolf Hitler. (Berlin 1936)

Michael Phelps swims to eight gold medals in a single Games. (Beijing 2008)

Seb Coe beats Steve Ovett to gold in the 1,500 metre final. (Moscow 1980)

Daley Thompson whistles on the podium. (Los Angeles 1984)

Source: *Sport Magazine*, www.sport-magazine.co.uk

10 insightful US sports facts*

1 **Michael Jordan is America's greatest athlete ever** – According to the ESPN *SportsCentury* retrospective, covering the 20th century. Baseball's Babe Ruth came in second.

2 **Babe Ruth wore a cabbage leaf under his cap to keep him cool when he played** – He changed it every two innings.

3 **Golfer Tiger Woods is the highest paid athlete in sport** – Between 1 June 2012 and 1 June 2013, he earned $78.1 million, $65 million of it from endorsements, according to *Forbes* magazine.

4 **The famous silhouette on the NBA logo belongs to Hall of Famer Jerry West** – The Los Angeles Laker, often referred to as 'The Logo' is depicted dribbling the ball up-court.

5 **Super Bowl XLVI (2012) was the most watched television programme in US history** – Some 111,346,000 people tuned in to see New York Giants beat New England Patriots 21-17.

6 **Three consecutive strikes in bowling is called a turkey** – The term a hangover from the days when, during Thanksgiving and Christma the bowling alley proprietor would award a turkey to the first persc to achieve three strikes.

7 **Sixty per cent of retired NBA players are bankrupt within five years** – According to a report by the *Toronto Star*. Famously, forme NBA MVP Allen Iverson 'went broke' despite earning more than $200 million in a celebrated career.

8 **On average, the action in a baseball game lasts 17 minutes 58 seconds** – According to *Wall Street Journal* research, which also claims the action time in an NFL game is just 11 minutes.

9 **The most dangerous sport for female Americans is cheerleading** Reports claim it accounts for two-thirds of all 'very serious injuries' the USA, where an estimated 3.6 million people take part.

10 **The greatest tale in American sport is probably this** – In 1962, San Francisco Giants manager Alvin Dark said: 'There'll be a man on the moon before [rookie pitcher] Gaylord Perry hits a home run.' Sever years later, on 20 July 1969, Neil Armstrong became the first man to set foot on the moon. And less than an hour later, Gaylord Perry struck his first home run, against the Los Angeles Dodgers.

Top 10 toughest Tour de France climbs*

CLIMB	SUMMIT	DISTANCE	AVERAGE GRADE
1 Col du Galibier	2,645 m (8,678 ft)	18.1 km (11.3 miles)	6.9%
2 Col du Tourmalet	2,115 m (6,939 ft)	17 km (10.6 miles)	7.4%
3 Alpe d'Huez	1,815 m (5,955 ft)	13.9 km (8.6 miles)	8.1%
4 Le Mont Ventoux	1,912 m (6,273 ft)	23 km (14.3 miles)	7.1%
5 Col d'Aubisque	1,709 m (5,607 ft)	18.4 km (11.4 miles)	6.4%
6 Col de la Madeleine	1,993 m (6,539 ft)	19.8 km (12.3 miles)	7.7%
7 Col d'Izoard	2,361 m (7,746 ft)	15.9 km (10 miles)	6.9%
8 Col du Glandon	1,924 m (6,312 ft)	21.6 km (13.4 miles)	5.1%
9 Col de Joux Plane	1,700 m (5,577 ft)	11.7 km (7.3 miles)	8.5%
10 Col de Peyresourde	1,569 m (5,148 ft)	15.27 km (9.5 miles)	6.1%

*As ranked by *www.cycling-challenge.com*

Source: www.cycling-challenge.com

Should you be wondering, 'col' translates as a pass between two mountain peaks.

10 notable world record football transfer fees

RECORD TRANSFER FEE	PLAYER	CLUBS	YEAR
1 **£100**	Willie Groves	West Bromwich Albion to Aston Villa	1893
2 **£1,000**	Alf Common	Sunderland to Middlesbrough	1905
3 **£5,000**	Syd Puddefoot	West Ham United to Falkirk	1922
4 **£52,000**	Hans Jeppson	Atalanta to Napoli	1952
5 **£152,000**	Luis Suárez	Barcelona to Internazionale	196
6 **£250,000**	Pietro Anastasi	Varese to Juventus	1968
7 **£1.2 million**	Giuseppe Savoldi	Bologna to Napoli	1975
8 **£5 million**	Diego Maradona	Barcelona to Napoli	1984
9 **£56 million**	Kaká	AC Milan to Real Madrid	2009
10 **£85 million***	Gareth Bale	Tottenham to Real Madrid	2013

*As at December 2013, the transfer fee paid for Bale is the latest world record. However, given that Real Madrid holds the last five record transfer fees (Bale, Ronaldo, Kaká, Zidane and Figo), the club may choose to break it again by the time you read this

10 full names of great Brazilian footballers

1. **Arthur Antunes Coimbra** – Zico

2. **Manuel Francisco dos Santos** – Garrincha

3. **Ronaldo de Assis Moreira** – Ronaldinho

4. **Eduardo Gonçalves de Andrade** – Tostão

5. **Jair Ventura Filho** – Jairzinho

6. **Marcos Evangelista de Moraes** – Cafu

7. **Ricardo Izecson dos Santos Leite** – Kaká

8. **Antônio de Oliveira Filho** – Careca

9. **Neymar da Silva Santos Júnior** – Neymar

10. **Sócrates Brasileiro Sampaio de Souza Vieira de Oliveira** – Sócrates

Tradition dictates that Brazil's greatest footballers are often known by something more catchy than their birth name – think Pelé rather than Edson Arantes do Nascimento.

Top 10 greatest footballers of all time*

PLAYER	NATIONAL TEAM/S	CLUB TEAM/S

1 **Alfredo Di Stéfano**   Argentina, Spain, Colombia   River Plate, Real Madrid

The original revolutionary: the European Cup would never have excited world football in the 1950s as it did without Real Madrid, who in turn, would not have dabbed it in stardust without the inspiration of Di Stéfano, the original perpetual motion match-winner.

2 **Pelé**   Brazil   Santos, New York Cosmos

Brazil's status as the world's top football nation was built on the triple World Cup glory of the era between 1958 and 1970 dominated by Edson Arantes do Nascimento, better known as Pelé, one of the greatest and most irresistible forces of nature ever to explode on the game.

3 **Diego Maradona**   Argentina   Boca Juniors, Barcelona, Napoli

No player has ever projected such a street urchin's dual genius for magic and mischief – highlighted by the extremes of the victorious 1986 World Cup when 'El Pibe de Oro' floored England with his most outrageous and most marvellous of goals.

4 **Franz Beckenbauer**   West Germany   Bayern Munich, New York Cosmos, Hamburg

Proof, as an attacking sweeper, that defenders can exert as creative a role as any forward.

5 **Johan Cruyff**   Netherlands   Ajax, Barcelona, Feyenoord

The heart and soul of the 1970s 'Total Football' innovation and a skills legacy that still lives on.

PLAYER	NATIONAL TEAM/S	CLUB TEAM/S

6 Lionel Messi Argentina Barcelona
Talent, temperament, goals and glory – and a rise up this list guaranteed as the titles pile up.

7 Ferenc Puskás Hungary, Spain Budapest Honvéd, Real Madrid
Left-footed goal-sharp who led football's international revival after the Second World War.

8 Bobby Charlton England Manchester United
Epitomized the best of British in the tradition of Bastin, Wright, Matthews and Finney.

9 Arthur Friedenreich Brazil Germania, Ypiranga, São Paulo, Flamengo
Brazil's original superstar in the 1920s who claimed the first haul of 1,000-plus goals.

10 Lev Yashin Soviet Union Dynamo Moscow
Hero of the old Soviet Union who brought acrobatic magic to the art of goalkeeping.

*According to Keir Radnedge, who has covered world football for more than 40 years and has written 35 books on the subject

Source: Keir Radnedge; follow him @KeirRadnedge and www.KeirRadnedge.com

Top 10 teams in the history of English football

TEAM	TOTAL POINTS*
1 Liverpool	324
2 Manchester United	315
3 Arsenal	207
4 Aston Villa	141
5 Everton	124
6 Chelsea	119.5
7 Tottenham Hotspur	101.5
8 Newcastle United	79.5
9 Manchester City	73
10 Sunderland	71

*Ranked by points calculated as follows: League title 10 points; the FA Cup title 5.5 points; League Cup title 4.5 points; European Cup 10 points; any other European trophy 6.5 points. One-off games, such as the Charity Shield and Super Cup, are not taken into account. Figures correct up to and including the 2012/13 season

Source: Sporting Intelligence, www.sportingintelligence.com

The 10 points awarded for a League title mean Manchester United are closing in on Liverpool at the top, while Chelsea and Manchester City are both expected to rise in the coming months.

Top 10 most successful nations in European football*

COUNTRY	WINNING CLUBS	TOTAL WINS†
1 **Spain**	Real Madrid 9, Barcelona 4	13
2 **England**	Liverpool 5, Manchester United 3, Nottingham Forest 2, Chelsea 1, Aston Villa 1	12
3 **Italy**	AC Milan 7, Internazionale 3, Juventus 2	12
4 **Germany**	Bayern Munich 5, Borussia Dortmund 1, SV Hamburg 1	7
5 **Netherlands**	Ajax 4, PSV Eindhoven 1, Feyenoord 1	6
6 **Portugal**	FC Porto 2, Benfica 2	4
7 **France**	Marseille	1
8 **Serbia**	Red Star Belgrade	1
9 **Romania**	Steaua Bucharest	1
10 **Scotland**	Celtic	1

*As at April 2014

†European Cup (1955/6 to 1991/2) and Champions League (1992/3 to end May 2013) victories. Where equal, countries are ranked in order of their most recent victory

10 very short managerial reigns

1 **44 days** (Brian Clough, Leeds United, 1974) – The short but infamous stint they made a film about, Brian Howard Clough arrived at Elland Road to take over from Don 'The Don' Revie, who had led Leeds to the League Championship the previous season and moved on to the England job. Clough made enemies of nearly everyone he encountered from the outset and was sacked after taking four points from a possible 12. He went to Nottingham Forest and went on to win two European Cups. P7 W1 D3 L3

2 **41 days** (Les Reed, Charlton Athletic, 2006) – Les Reed's 41-day stint as manager at the Valley saw him win just once and oversee a Carling Cup defeat to League Two Wycombe Wanderers. The man they nicknamed 'Les Misérables' was sacked on Christmas Eve and replaced by Alan Pardew. P8 W1 D1 L6

3 **40 days** (Alex McLeish, Nottingham Forest, 2012/13) – Fresh from taking Birmingham City down into the Championship, McLeish replaced Sean O'Driscoll with the brief of taking Forest up into the Premier League. He lasted 40 days, a disagreement with the Kuwait owners over transfer policy leading to his departure by mutual consent. P7 W1 D2 L4

4 **33 days** (Steve Coppell, Manchester City, 1996) – In between spells in charge at Crystal Palace, Coppell took the job at Manchester City. Back then, City were synonymous with epic underachievement. Coppell left after six games, citing stress. P6 W2 D1 L3

5 **28 days** (Paul Hart, Queen's Park Rangers, 2009/10) – Only ever a stopgap appointment, yet few expected Paul Hart to be done and dusted at Loftus Road in less than a month. Bar, perhaps, the itchy-fingered owner, Flavio Briatore. Hart left by 'mutual consent'. P5 W1 D2 L2

6 **13 days** (Micky Adams, Swansea City, 1997) – Swansea City went through six managers inside 18 months in the 1990s, with Micky Adams lasting less than two weeks. He walked away after promises for funds failed to materialize. Astonishingly, though, he wasn't the club's shortest-standing manager during that period (see No. 8). P3 W0 D0 L3

7 **9 days** (Martin Ling, Cambridge United, 2009) – Taking the job after his predecessor quit following 'issues' with the chairman, Ling took over at the Conference National club and lasted all of nine days. He, too, had irreconcilable differences with the man at the top. P0 W0 D0 L0. (Ling later returned following the departure of the club's chairman and managed the club for 87 games.)

8 **7 days** (Kevin Cullis, Swansea City, 1996) – In and out at Swansea City in just over a week and two games. Cullis was either unceremoniously sacked or he resigned, depending on who you listen to. P2 W0 D0 L2

9 **4 days** (Dave Bassett, Crystal Palace, 1984) – In the job so short a length of time, Dave 'Harry' Bassett hadn't even signed a contract at Palace before changing his mind and heading back to Wimbledon. P0 W0 D0 L0

10 **10 minutes** (Leroy Rosenior, Torquay United, 2007) – Appointed just as a consortium took the club over, and when the ink on the deal was dry, they wanted their own man. In and out inside 600 seconds. A record unlikely to be beaten. P0 W0 D0 L0

Accurate as at 5 September 2013, though the preposterous nature of modern football and its clubs' blood-thirsty owners may soon add new entries to this list.

10 unusual football transfer 'fees'

1 **Two tonnes of meat** – Ion Radu transferred from Jiul Petrosani to Valcea in 1998. The club's president explained: 'We will sell the meat, then pay all the other players' salaries.'

2 **A set of kit, bag of balls and a goal net** – Gary Pallister transferred from Billingham Town to Middlesbrough in 1984. Manchester United paid £2.3 million for Pallister five years later.

3 **A player's weight in fresh shrimp** – Kenneth Kristensen transferred from Vindbjart to Floey in 2002. Kristensen was said to have weighed in at around the 75 kg (165 lb) mark.

4 **30 tracksuits** – Zat Knight transferred from Rushall Olympic to Fulham in 1999. The tracksuits were more a gesture of goodwill than a transfer fee.

5 **£100 and a barrel of beer** – Ernie Blenkinsop transferred from Cudworth to Hull City in 1921. Said barrel was said to contain 45 litres (80 pints) of unspecified brown booze.

6 **A set of weights** – Ian Wright transferred from Greenwich Borough to Crystal Palace in 1985. Six years and 117 goals later, Wright signed for Arsenal and represented England.

7 **A set of football kit** –John Barnes transferred from Sudbury Court to Watford in 1981. Five years later, Liverpool paid Watford £900,000 for Barnes.

8 **10 footballs** –Liviu Baicea transferred from Jiul Petrosani to UT Arad in 1998. Having swapped one player for meat (see No. 1), Jiul Petrosani's president opted for a slightly more appropriate trade here.

9 **A freezer full of ice cream** – Hugh McLenahan transferred from Stockport County to Manchester United in 1928. United assistant Louis Rocca ran an ice cream business at the time.

10 **15 kg (33 lb) of pork sausages** – Marius Cioara transferred from UT Arad to Regal Hornia in 2006. Ciora retired a day after this deal, claiming 'it was a huge insult', leaving Regal Hornia to demand the sausages back.

10 famous people who could have been footballers

SPORT

Karol Józef Wojtyła – Said to be a accomplished goalkeeper during his youth, turning out for his university side in Krakow. But the future Pope John Paul II had his head turned by the big man upstairs.

Sir David Frost – Caught the eye of a Nottingham Forest scout, scoring eight times in a single game, but chose an education at Cambridge University over the beautiful game, then followed a career as a broadcaster.

Rod Stewart – Reportedly on the books at Brentford, but evidently not for long. Became a multi-million-selling pop star, via a stint as a grave digger.

Perry 'Billy Mitchell' Fenwick – Before being lured by the whiff of greasepaint and the Queen Victoria's odd own-brand lager, the actor who plays *EastEnder* Billy Mitchell had a trial at Leyton Orient.

Julio Iglesias – The dashing Spaniard was another goalkeeper, good enough to be on the books of Real Madrid. A car accident put paid to those plans; fortunately for the singer, his larynx escaped in full working order.

Audley Harrison – The Olympic super heavyweight boxing champion could have been a footballing contender, having had a trial at Watford.

Albert Camus – The philosopher plied his other trade between the posts for Racing Universitaire Algérois before following a more cerebral path, but still remarked 'All that I know most surely about morality and obligations, I owe to football.'

Gordon Ramsay – The volatile chef was once a triallist at Glasgow Rangers, but a knee injury put paid to his hopes of making it as a footballer.

Luciano Pavarotti – Before becoming far too lumpy to leap around, the young Pavarotti was a goalkeeper who had trials with his local team in Modena.

Sean Connery – The future James Bond reportedly turned down an offer to join Manchester United, having already committed himself to a tour with the musical *South Pacific*.

SPORT

10 famous football clubs who changed their names

1 **Everton** were **St Domingo**

2 **Cardiff City** were **Riverside**

3 **Bristol Rovers** were **Black Arabs**

4 **Manchester City** were **Ardwick**

5 **Newcastle United** were **Stanley**

6 **West Ham United** were **Thames Iron Works**

7 **Queen's Park Rangers** were **St Jude's**

8 **AC Milan** were **Milan Cricket and Foot-Ball Club**

9 **Arsenal** were **Dial Square**

10 **Birmingham City** were **Small Heath Alliance**

0 memorable football club names

FL Fart – A Norwegian football club founded in 1934 and located in Vang, should you go looking for them.

Flying Camel – Taiwan's national champions in 1983, 1984 and 1985, now sadly disbanded. They were also known as Fei To, but that's not even mildly amusing.

Bangkok Bravo FC – The full name? Amon Rattanakosin Krung Thep Mahanakhon Mahinthara Mahadilok Phop Noppharat Ratchathani Ayuthaya Burirom Udomratchaniwet Mahasathan Amon Piman Awatan Sathit Sakkathattiya Witsanukam Prasit Bravo Association Football Club. An understandable rebranding, then.

The Botswana Meat Commission FC – Founded in 1969 and competing in the Botswana Premier League. Nicknamed 'the Meat Men', but without explanation.

Club Atlético Chaco For Ever – Generally shortened to Chaco For Ever, this Argentine outfit followed the tradition of being influenced by the English. Boca went for 'Juniors'; Chaco went for the first thing they could think of.

Club Deportivo Morón – Argentine football club based in Buenos Aires, founded in 1947 and currently playing in the Primera B Metropolitana. The Spanish *morón* translates far less amusingly as 'hummock', as in a small mound or hillock.

Young Boys – Officially, Berner Sport Club Young Boys 1898, but more commonly abbreviated to a name which no doubt sounded less questionable when the club was formed in, yes, 1898. The Young Boys play at Bern's Stade de Suisse Wankdorf, which is equally regrettable.

PAOK FC – More practical than in any way amusing, the official name of this Greek club is Panthessaloníkios Athlitikós Ómilos Konstantinoupolitón. Thank them for making it easy.

Deportivo Wanka – It was either this lot or Zimbabwean outfit Wankie FC. Deportivo edged it for being nicknamed 'Los Wankeros'.

King Faisal Babies – Of Ghana.

161

10 best footballers never to play in a World Cup finals

1 **Alfredo Di Stéfano** – Turned out for Argentina, Colombia and Spain but missed out due to politics (Argentina refusing to enter in 1950 and FIFA ruling him ineligible in 1954), by Spain failing to qualify and by injury striking when they finally did in 1962.

2 **George Best** – Represented Northern Ireland 37 times between 1964 and 1977, but neither he nor his nation graced any of the three World Cup finals that took place during that time. By the time they reached the final in 1982, Best was a spent force.

3 **Duncan Edwards** – The Manchester United midfielder made his England debut in 1955 and was expected to lead his country to World Cup glory. Tragically, he was one of 23 men who died in the Munich air disaster in 1958, aged just 21.

4 **Bernd Schuster** – Creative powerhouse for club (Barcelona, most notably) and country, Schuster won the 1980 European Championships with West Germany but retired within four years, aged 24, after disagreements with the German FA.

5 **Ryan Giggs** – The most decorated footballer in English football, but held back in the Welsh team by a series of inferior team-mates. Had he played in the same team as Ian Rush, Mark Hughes and Neville Southall, three other Welshmen who never reached the final, he wouldn't be on this list.

Matthew Le Tissier – Remarkably gifted but restricted to eight appearances for England, his way blocked by Gazza and a suspicion that he was too much of a luxury for international football. If nothing else, his penalties would have helped.

George Weah – FIFA World Player of the Year, European Footballer of the Year, star for AC Milan, but saddled with a national team (Liberia) who would never grace the game's greatest stage.

Liam Brady – Capped 72 times for his country but 'Chippy' never took part in the game's biggest tournament. He might have, had he not retired during qualification for the final in 1990, which the Republic of Ireland reached.

Jari Litmanen – Cultured attacking midfielder for Ajax, Litmanen was Finland's greatest ever footballer, although that's damning with the faintest of praise. Sadly, he alone couldn't carry a clap-trap collective to the World Cup finals.

Eric Cantona – Sadly for Cantona, he played for France when they were too shabby to qualify. When they did improve, Zinedine Zidane provided all the creativity they needed.

10 most memorable footballer endorsements

1 Viagra – 'Talk to your doctor... I would.' Pelé, the most famous footballer of all time, trots out the most famous lines in footballer ad history, extolling the benefits of popping penis pills.

2 Brut – At the height of his fame/money-making powers, 'Mighty Mouse' Kevin Keegan teamed up with loveable pugilist 'Enry Cooper to very memorably splash a cheap aftershave all over.

3 The Green Cross Code – And about the same time, Kevin Keegan's agent booked him to appear as the face behind a public service advert educating kids on the safest way to cross the roads. He also apparently found time to play some football.

4 Casillero Del Diablo – Endorsed by Manchester United. 'Guys. Wehavea. Problem,' warns Wayne Rooney in an advert for Spanish wine, with the conviction of a door. 'The boss says. That. A new De is a... rriving... They say. He is a... Legend.' A masterclass in what can go wrong when footballers are asked to memorize words.

5 Prophylactics – One of football's least likely sex symbols, that didn stop Ronaldinho, the buck-toothed Brazilian, launching his own range of condoms. Confusingly named 'Sex Free', they feature the slogan 'Eu Sou Galo', which means 'I am Galo' – the nickname of hi club, Atlético Mineiro.

6 The Local Pub – Bobby Moore starred in an advert in which the only Englishman ever to lift the World Cup stops in at his local pub on the way home to get tanked up on East End booze and humilia his wife at darts. Brought to you by, we assume, the British Beer Trade, and unexpected to say the least.

Pizza Hut – Three men, Stuart Pearce, Chris Waddle and Gareth Southgate, whose penalty misses had ensured England crashed out of the 1990 World Cup and 1996 European Championships when on the brink of glory, team up to cash in by eating pizza and repeatedly crowbarring the word 'miss' into their conversation.

Unipart – Pat Jennings, the world-renowned goalkeeper, dressed up as an oil filter? Diving left and right to save a series of oily rags? Things were more innocent back then.

Paddy Power – One minute the male star of this advert is enjoying a candlelit bath with his wife, the next she disappears under the water and in her place pops Carlton Palmer. 'Isn't this nice, just you and Carlton Palmer, having a bath,' growls the gangly ex pro, before handing the man some money and imploring him to stick some Chris de Burgh on.

Sugar Puffs – And here he is again, Kevin Keegan this time cashing in during his Newcastle United days in an advert for a sugar-heavy breakfast cereal. The story – a Wembley final is heading to extra-time when Kev sends on 'the big man', Honey Monster. Seconds later he powers home the winner with a towering header! A tactical masterstroke from Keegan to secure a piece of silverware? Unlikely.

10 less gifted brothers of famous footballers

1 Hugo Maradona – Brother of Diego, arguably the greatest player on the planet. Midfielder Hugo played for a number of clubs you'll have never heard of – Progreso, Avispa Fukuoka and on and on. Their other brother, Raúl, a striker, turned out for Deportivo Municipal and Deportivo Laferrere.

2 Carl Hoddle – Less creative and celebrated brother of Glenn, the future misunderstood manager of England. While Glenn found fame and fortune with Tottenham and Monaco, Carl left White Hart Lane to join Leyton Orient before quietly ending his career at Barnet.

3 Giuseppe Baresi – A midfielder skilled enough to play almost 400 times for Internazionale and 18 times for the Italian national team. Sadly for Giuseppe, the world remembers his brother Franco the most gifted defender in Italian football history for AC Milan and the Azzurri.

4 François Ribéry – While older brother Franck rampages down the wing for Bayern Munich and France, François has struggled to make such an impact – his career high coming with Aviron Bayonnais FC in the Championnat National, France's third tier.

5 Dave Sansom – His brother Kenny made the left-back role his own for Arsenal and England. Dave hit the heights of Fisher Athletic and Barnet.

Michael Rummenigge – The younger Rummenigge played more than 300 Bundesliga games for Bayern and Borussia Dortmund, earning two caps for his country. Alas, all anyone really remembers him for is being the brother of Karl-Heinz Rummenigge, one of Germany's greatest ever strikers.

Christopher Kanu – His older brother Nwankwo made his name at Arsenal and for Nigeria. Christopher, a defender, struggled to make much of a mark – released by Ajax, he ended up at Eagle Cement, via Top Oss, Peterborough United and Wingate & Finchley.

Patrick Makélélé – His brother Claude found fame and fortune as the legs and lungs of Real Madrid and France, winning World Cups and European Championships. Patrick's career as a midfielder was more modest, with spells at two clubs we've never heard of: FC Melun and Le Mée.

Mutlu Özil – Arsenal and Germany midfielder Mesut followed in the footsteps of older brother, Mutlu, whose career was less glittering – the striker's high point came at lesser-known German outfit FirtinaSpor Gelsenkirchen 1995.

Joel Cantona – While brother Eric was kicking out at crowds and talking about trawlers, Joel, a defender, was playing for CS Meaux, Peterborough United and Stockport County.

Top 10 greatest cricketers of all time*

1 **Don Bradman** (Australia) – Just 1.7 m (5 ft 7 in), but still head and shoulders above any batsman in the history of the game. His Test average of 99.94 may just be the most impressive statistic in all sport, and England were so worried by his genius in the 1932/3 Ashes tour that they devised an entire system – Bodyline – to deal with him.

2 **Garry Sobers** (West Indies) – If Bradman was cricket's batsman nonpareil, Sobers was its greatest all-rounder. A flamboyant left-hander who was the first man to hit six sixes in a first-class over (in 1968), he also switched effortlessly between seam and spin, and caught pretty well everything that came his way. And he often did it all on a couple of hours' sleep.

3 **Shane Warne** (Australia) – Often credited with revitalizing the arcane art of leg-spin, but the truth is Warne was inimitable. His first ball in Ashes cricket – a ridiculous leg-break to bowl Mike Gatting at Old Trafford in 1993 – was the mother of all calling cards, and he finished with an astonishing 708 Test wickets and an indelible place in the bad dreams of English batsmen.

4 **Jack Hobbs** (England) – Modest, self-effacing and utterly correct, Hobbs was revered as 'The Master' – a reference to his unprecedented tally of 197 first-class hundreds as much as it was to the air of inevitability that descended when he walked to the crease for Surrey or in 61 Test matches for England between 1908 and 1930. He was also a demon in the covers in an age where fielding was considered a little *infra dig*.

5 **Viv Richards** (West Indies) – Between 1974 and 1981, in an era of helmets, Viv – everyone called him Viv – wore a maroon cap, yet still treated the fastest bowlers with utter contempt. Here was the ultimate intimidating batsman, a man who swaggered his way to the middle and bristled with affront at the notion that a bowler might be trying to ruin his day. He usually ruined theirs.

Sachin Tendulkar (India) – India's 'Little Master' began his Test career in the late 1980s; in 2012, he became the first man to score 100 international hundreds. In between, countless other careers began and ended – but Tendulkar just kept going until his retirement in November 2013, the most worshipped single cricketer in the history of the game.

Brian Lara (West Indies) – Not content with holding the Test record for the highest individual score on one occasion, he then recaptured it with his unbeaten 400 against England in Antigua in 2003/4. If Tendulkar was the most reliable, Lara was the most watchable. His exaggerated backlift was one of the signature gestures of modern batsmanship.

W. G. Grace (England) – Cricket's first superstar, W. G. may also have been Victorian England's first celebrity. If his gamesmanship seemed out of kilter with the mores of the time, then his status was undeniable, and he is widely regarded as the father of modern batsmanship.

Sydney Barnes (England) – He played the last of his 27 Tests in 1914, but S. F. Barnes may just have been the most skilful seam bowler in all of cricket: a tally of 189 wickets for England at an average of 16 scarcely dispels the notion. He was renowned for his grumpiness, but probably more famous for his brisk leg-cutters.

Muttiah Muralitharan (Sri Lanka) – It's hard to see how any bowler will ever surpass Murali's total of 800 Test wickets, taken between 1992 and 2010; and even though cleared by the ICC, it's equally tricky to see an end to questions over the legality of his bowling action. What is undeniable is that he almost singlehandedly made Sri Lanka a competitive force.

*According to Lawrence Booth, the editor of *Wisden Cricketers' Almanack* and a cricket writer for the *Daily Mail*. He tweets @the_topspin

10 most memorable cricketing 'sledges'

1 **Glen McGrath and Eddo Brandes** – Unable to dismiss the little-known Zimbabwean batsman Brandes, McGrath asked, 'Why are you so fat?' Brandes replied, 'Because every time I f**k your wife, she gives me a biscuit.'

2 **Mark Waugh and James Ormond** – As the uncelebrated Englishma Ormond entered the field, Australia's Mark 'brother of the superior Steve' Waugh, standing at slip, piped up, 'Mate, what are you doing out here? There's no way you're good enough to play for England!' Ormond's instant response cut deep. 'Maybe so, but at least I'm the best player in my family.'

3 **Spectator and Phil Tufnell** – During the Ashes of 1990/91, Phil 'the Cat' Tufnell approached the boundary to assume his fielding position. A spectator piped up: 'Oi, Tufnell. Lend us your brain, we'r building an idiot!'

4 **Vic Richardson and Douglas Jardine** – In one of several versions of a now legendary exchange during the infamous Bodyline Ashes to of 1932, England's captain Jardine banged on the Australian dressir room door, affronted at having been called a 'bastard' out on the field. Australia's vice-captain Richardson answered the door, heard Jardine's complaint, then turned back to his team-mates and asked 'OK, which of you bastards called this bastard a bastard?'

5 **Rod Marsh and Ian Botham** – During an Ashes match, Botham arrived at the wicket, where Aussie wicketkeeper Marsh was waitin Marsh: 'So, how's your wife and my kids?' Botham: 'Wife's fine. Kids are retarded.'

Merv Hughes and Viv Richards – During a Test match in Jamaica, with Hughes eyeballing Richards after every delivery, the host skipper growled: 'Don't you be staring at me, man. This is my island, my culture. And in my culture we just bowl.' Hughes' response was to the point: 'In my culture we just say f**k off.'

Merv Hughes and Robin Smith – Having bowled a succession of balls the English batsman couldn't get near, Hughes offered Smith some advice: 'If you turn the bat over you'll get the instructions, mate.'

Fred Trueman and Raman Subba Row – With Trueman bowling, the ball was hit out towards Row, fielding at slip, but flew between the hapless fielder's legs. At the end of the over, Row ran across and said: 'Sorry Fred, I should've kept my legs closed.' 'So should your mother,' replied Trueman.

Merv Hughes and Javed Miandad – During a Test match in 1991, Pakistan's Miandad attempted to unsettle the sledger's sledger, calling the moustachioed Aussie a 'big, fat bus conductor'. A few balls later, Merv took Miandad's wicket, and as he ran past in celebration, shouted: 'Tickets please!'

Viv Richards and Greg Thomas – Bowling to Richards in a county match, Thomas watched several balls fly past the great Jamaican's bat. Buoyed by the sight, Thomas let rip. 'It's red, it's round and it weighs five ounces, in case you were wondering.' Richards held his tongue, then hit the next ball straight out of the ground before responding: 'You know what it looks like now go and get it.'

Top 10 most inept Test scores

TEST SCORE	MATCH*/DATE	LOCATION
1 26 all out (27 overs)	**New Zealand** vs. England, 1st Test, 25 Mar 1955	Auckland New Zealand
=2 30 all out (18.4 overs)	**South Africa** vs. England, 1st Test, 13 Feb 1896	Port Elizabeth South Africa
=2 30 all out (12.3 overs)	England vs. **South Africa**, 1st Test, 14 Jun 1924	Birmingham, UK
4 35 all out (22.4 overs)	**South Africa** vs. England, 1st Test, 1 Apr 1899	Cape Town South Africa
=5 36 all out (23 overs)	England vs. **Australia**, 1st Test, 29 May 1902	Birmingham, UK
=5 36 all out (23.2 overs)	Australia vs. **South Africa**, 1st Test, 12 Feb 1932	Melbourne Australia
=7 42 all out (39 overs)	**New Zealand** vs. Australia, 1st Test, 29 Mar 1946	Wellington New Zealand
=7 42 all out (37.3 overs)	**Australia** vs. England, 1st Test, 10 Feb 1888	Sydney, Australia
=7 42 all out (17 overs)	England vs. **India**, 1st Test, 20 Jun 1974	London, UK
10 43 all out (28.2 overs)	**South Africa** vs. England, 1st Test, 25 Mar 1889	Cape Town South Africa

*Team with low score in bold

Top 10 greatest Formula One drivers*

DRIVER/COUNTRY	WORLD CHAMPIONSHIP TITLES	RACES	WINS	WIN PERCENTAGE
1 **Juan Manuel Fangio** (Argentina)	5	51	24	47.05
2 **Alberto Ascari** (Italy)	2	32	13	40.6
3 **Jim Clark** (Scotland)	2	72	25	34.7
4 **Sebastian Vettel** (Germany)	4	120	39	32.5
5 **Michael Schumacher** (Germany)	7	308	91	29.5
6 **Jackie Stewart** (Scotland)	3	100	27	27
7 **Alain Prost** (France)	4	200	51	25.5
8 **Ayrton Senna** (Brazil)	3	162	41	25.3
9 **Stirling Moss** (England)	0	66	16	24.2
10 **Damon Hill** (England)	1	122	22	18.03

*Ranked by win percentage of drivers who have raced a minimum of ten F1 races. Figures correct as at November 2013

10 notable tennis records*

1 **Most titles in the Open era†** – Jimmy Connors, 109.

2 **Most victories in the Open era** – Jimmy Connors, 1,243. Martina Navratilova holds the women's record with 1,442 victories.

3 **Most all-time Grand Slam victories** – Roger Federer, 17 (Australian Open 4, French Open 1, Wimbledon 7, US Open 5).

4 **The only Grand Slam winner‡ during the Open era** – Rod Laver (1969).

5 **Most consecutive weeks ranked No. 1** – Roger Federer, 237 (from February 2004 to August 2008).

6 **Most total weeks ranked No. 1** – Roger Federer, 287.

7 **Longest Open era winning streak** – Guillermo Vilas, 46 matches (1977).

8 **Longest game** – 11 hours 5 minutes (John Isner vs. Nicolas Mahut, Wimbledon 1st Round 2010, 6-4, 3-6, 6-7 (7-9), 7-6 (7-3), 70-68, played out over three days).

9 **Most aces in a single match** – John Isner, 113 (vs. Nicolas Mahut, Wimbledon 1st Round 2010).

10 **Fastest serve** – Sam Groth, 263 km/h (163.4 mph) (2012). The women's record is held by Venus Williams at 207.6 km/h (129 mph) (2007).

*As at November 2013

†The 'Open era' of tennis began in 1968, when professionals were allowed to enter the Grand Slams. Prior to 1968, these were open only to amateurs

‡A player who holds the men's four singles titles of Australian Open, French Open, Wimbledon and US Open at the same time

Top 10 pound-for-pound boxers ever*

BOXER	WON/LOST/DREW	FOUGHT

1 Sugar Ray Robinson W 173 (KO 108), L 19 (KO 1), D 6 1940–65
The pound-for-pound greatest fighting machine in history.

2 Muhammad Ali W 56 (KO 37), L 5 (KO 1), D 0 1960–81
Arguably has the best résumé of any fighter and fought the best for 20 years.

3 Henry Armstrong W 150 (KO 101), L 21 (KO 2), D 10 1931–45
Reigned in three weight classes at the same time.

4 Sugar Ray Leonard W 36 (KO 25), L 3 (KO 1), D 1 1977–97
The perfect blend of speed and intelligence.

5 Joe Louis W 66 (KO 52), L 3 (KO 2), D 0 1934–51
Dominant heavyweight king and a devastating finisher.

6 Roberto Durán W 103 (KO 70), L 16 (KO 4), D 0 1968–2001
Was rightly feared from lightweight to super middleweight.

7 Harry Greb W 162 (KO 48), L 17 (KO 2), D 19 1913–26
Vicious middleweight champion who fought anyone and everyone.

8 Willie Pep W 229 (KO 65), L 11 (KO 6), D 1 1940–66
Defensive master and owner of the myth that he was the only fighter to win a round without throwing a punch.

9 Archie Moore W 185 (KO 131), L 23 (KO 7), D 10 1935–63
Light-heavyweight general who had to wait too long for his shot, but still held the title from age 36–46.

10 Jimmy Wilde W 131 (KO 99), L 3, D 2 1911–23
Britain's best, the Welshman was dubbed 'The Mighty Atom'.

---

*According to Tris Dixon, editor of *Boxing News*

Source: Tris Dixon, *Boxing News*, www.boxingnewsonline.net

10 notable London Prize Ring Rules

1 That on the men being stripped, it shall be the duty of the seconds to examine their drawers, and if any objection arise as to insertion of improper substances therein, they shall appeal to their umpires, who, with the concurrence of the referee, shall direct what alterations shall be made.

2 No spikes be used in fighting boots except those authorized by the Pugilistic Benevolent Association, which shall not exceed three-eights of an inch from the sole of the boot, and shall not be less than one-eight of an inch broad at the point; and, it shall be in the power of the referee to alter, or file in any way he pleases, spikes which shall not accord with the above dimensions, even to filing them away altogether.

3 That it shall be 'a fair stand-up fight', and if either man shall wilfully throw himself down without receiving a blow, whether blows shall have previously been exchanged or not, he shall be deemed to have lost the battle; but that this rule shall not apply to a man who in a close slips down from the grasp of his opponent to avoid punishment, or from obvious accident or weakness.

4 That butting with the head shall be deemed foul, and the party resorting to this practice shall be deemed to have lost the battle.

5 That a blow struck when a man is thrown or down, shall be deemed foul. That a man with one knee and one hand on the ground, or with both knees on the ground, shall be deemed down; and a blow given in either of those positions shall be considered foul, providing always, that when in such position, the man so down shall not himself strike or attempt to strike.

That a blow struck below the waistband shall be deemed foul, and that, in a close, seizing an antagonist below the waist, by the thigh, or otherwise, shall be deemed foul.

That all attempts to inflict injury by gouging, or tearing the flesh with the fingers or nails, and biting, shall be deemed foul.

That kicking, or deliberately falling on an antagonist, with the knees or otherwise when down, shall be deemed foul.

That the use of hard substances, such as stones, or sticks, or of resin, in the hand during the battle shall be deemed foul, and that on the requisition of the seconds, of either man, the accused shall open his hands for the examination of the referee.

That in the event of magisterial or other interference, or in case of darkness coming on, the referee shall have the power to name the time and place for the next meeting, if possible, on the same day, or as soon after as may be.

These London Prize Ring Rules were introduced in 1838 by the British Pugilists' Protective Association to improve safety in the ring. They were revised in 1853 (the version abridged here) and again in 1866, before being replaced by the more stringent Marquess of Queensbury Rules the following year.

10 boxing bouts that ended unexpectedly

1 **Adolph Wolgast vs. Joe Rivers** (4 July 1912) – In the 13th round of his lightweight title defence with Rivers in Los Angeles, the hard-hitting Wolgast landed the knockout blow – just as Rivers was landing one of his own, leaving both men sprawled on the canvas. Wolgast was awarded the fight for attempting to rise first before the ten count was complete, although he was supposedly aided by the referee and outrage duly ensued.

2 **Jack Dempsey vs. Jack Sharkey** (21 June 1927) – Complaining to the referee about a low blow in the seventh round, Sharkey was unable to admire the sweet left hand Dempsey landed on his chin to drop him to the canvas. When the little tweeting birdies finally lifted from above his head, the fight was over and the arguments had begun. A rematch followed, where Sharkey had his revenge.

3 **Roberto Durán vs. Ken Buchanan** (26 June 1972) – Few would disagree that the legendary Durán was worthy of victory against the WBA World Lightweight Champion Buchanan, but the blow that ended the fight seemed low to everyone watching – bar the referee. He awarded him one of boxing's most contentious KOs.

4 **Sugar Ray Leonard vs. Roberto Durán** (25 November 1980) – The most infamous and unexpected TKO in boxing history, Durán had won the first fight between the two five months earlier to take the welterweight title. This time, largely outclassed for seven and a half rounds, the champion shocked the world by turning his back and refusing to fight on. He supposedly cried '*no mas*' ('no more'), and blamed it on stomach cramps.

5 **Steve McCarthy vs. Tony Wilson** (21 September 1989) – The end appeared nigh for former British Light Heavyweight Champion Wilson, pinned to the ropes in the third amid a barrage of blows from his unbeaten opponent. Finally, the knockout blow arrived – delivered, quite unexpectedly, by Tony Wilson's mother. Entering the ring, she struck her son's assailant on the head with the heel of her shoe. When a bloodied McCarthy refused to re-enter the ring, Wilson was awarded the fight on a TKO.

Julio César Chávez vs. Meldrick Taylor (17 March 1990) – Leading after 11 rounds, Taylor needed only survive the 12th to take this junior welterweight unification fight. And even when the dangerous Chávez knocked him to the canvas late on, he climbed to his feet and raised his gloves, aware that he'd done enough with two seconds left on the clock. Strangely, the referee saw it differently, deciding he was in no fit state to continue and declaring Chávez the winner.

Riddick Bowe vs. Andrew Golota (11 July 1996) – Bad blood was visible when heavyweight heavy favourite Bowe and the largely unknown Golota met at Madison Square Garden. After Golota was disqualified for low blows, Bowe's entourage invaded the ring and cracked the Pole on the head with a walkie-talkie, opening a gash that required 11 stitches and kick-starting a full-blown riot in the ring. When they met again that December, Golota was disqualified again for yet more low blows.

Lennox Lewis vs. Oliver McCall (6 February 1997) – Meeting again three years after McCall upset Lewis for the heavyweight title, the Brit made all the running during the first four rounds and seemed set to gain his revenge. But then, in the fifth, a strange thing happened: McCall suddenly burst into tears and made no attempt to defend himself, leaving the referee with no alternative but to call a confused end to the fight. Mental issues were later blamed.

Evander Holyfield vs. Mike Tyson (28 June 1997) – A rematch of their epic heavyweight title fight of the previous year, won by the challenger Holyfield, Tyson surprised everyone, particularly Holyfield, by chewing on his right ear and earning himself a two-point deduction. When the fight restarted, Iron Mike clamped on again, this time taking a large chunk out of Holyfield's left ear. Disqualified, he was later fined $3 million and had his boxing licence revoked for a year and sanity questioned.

Floyd Mayweather vs. Victor Ortiz (17 September 2011) – When Ortiz attempted to headbutt 'Money' Mayweather and was docked a point, the fight was paused for everyone to regain their composure. The fighters touched gloves but, while the ref wasn't even watching, let alone telling them to box, Mayweather caught Ortiz with a swift, decisive one-two, knocking him to the canvas for the count. Against the spirit of the sport, no question, but entirely legal.

Top 10 golf courses

GOLF COURSE/LOCATION	YEAR BUILT	PAR	LENGTH
1 Pine Valley (New Jersey, USA)	1918	70	6,999 yd (6,400 m
2 Augusta National (Georgia, USA)	1933	72	6,925 yd (6,332 m
3 Cypress Point (California, USA)	1928	72	6,524 yd (5,965 m
4 Turnberry Resort: Ailsa Course (Ayrshire, Scotland)	1946	70	7,211 yd (6,594 m
5 Shinnecock Hills (New York, USA)	1891	70	6,813 yd (6,223 m
6 Kingston Heath (Melbourne, Australia)	1909	72	6,352 yd (5,808 m
7 Pebble Beach (California, USA)	1919	72	7,040 yd (6,437 m
8 Royal Birkdale (Lancashire, England)	1894	72	6,817 yd (6,233 m
9 Royal County Down: Championship Course (County Down, Northern Ireland)	1889	71	7,245 yd (6,587 m
10 Muirfield (East Lothian, Scotland)	1891	71	7,245 yd (6,625 m

Source: *Golf World* magazine

10 notable golf records*

Most Majors – Jack Nicklaus, 18 (1962–86: Masters 6, US Open 4, Open Championship 3, US PGA Championship 5).

Longest drive on the PGA Tour – Carl Cooper, 787 yd (719.6 m) (1992 Texas Open). Cooper's drive, which benefited from running down a cart path, was not recognized by the PGA as it was not made on one of the two designated holes used for recording longest drives during that tournament. The longest recorded drive was Mike Austin's 515 yd (470.9 m) in the US National Senior Open Championship in 1974.

Most runner-ups in Majors – Jack Nicklaus, 19.

Most runner-ups in Majors without winning one – Colin Montgomerie, 5.

Most Ryder Cup appearances – Nick Faldo, 11 (GB and Ireland and Europe, 1977–97). Faldo also holds the record of most points won, at 25.

Most Open Championship wins – Harry Vardon, 6.

Most Augusta green jackets – Jack Nicklaus, 6.

Largest career earnings – Tiger Woods has earned well over $100 million in his career, a figure sure to have gone up by the time you read this. Compare and contrast with Jack Nicklaus, who won 'just' $5.7 million in his career.

PGA Tour career wins – Sam Snead, 82.

Most consecutive weeks ranked No. 1 – Tiger Woods, 281 (12 June 2005–30 October 2010). Woods also tops the list of most total weeks at the top of the world rankings with 652. (Next best: Greg Norman, 331.)

*As at November 2013

10 strangest golf courses on (and off) the planet

1 **Mission Hills Icon Course** (Shenzehen, China) – Semi-serious crazy golf. Currently under construction, it's a regular golf course with massive pandas, the Great Wall of China weaving through it and one green sitting slap-bang in the middle of a giant noodle bowl.

2 **Nullarbor Links** (Nullarbor Plain, Australia) – Eighteen holes spread out across 1,365 km (848 miles), 18 towns and two time zones, along Australia's Nullarbor Plain, from Kalgoorlie in Western Australia to Ceduna in the south. Ditch the buggy, take a car.

3 **Merapi Golf Course** (Java, Indonesia) – An impressive course laid out in the foothills of Mount Merapi, a large volcano that overshadows the course in more ways than one. When it last erupted, in late 2010, it spat vast dollops of molten lava across the course, which redefined the term 'natural hazard'.

4 **Prison View Golf Course** (Louisiana State Penitentiary, Angola, USA) – So named because it sits inside the largest maximum security prison in the USA. You'll need to allow 48 hours for a background check before scheduling a tee time. And if the threat of criminal inmates wasn't enough to contend with, the course also boasts alligators and rattlesnakes.

5 **Camp Bonifas** (Panmunjom, South Korea) – A one-hole par-3 affair you'll find close to one of the most heavily fortified borders in the world, sat just 400 m (440 yd) from the Korean Demilitarized Zone. Tread carefully as the hole has minefields bordering it on three sides.

SPORT

Lost City Golf Course (Sun City, South Africa) – It pays to play a more conservative approach on the 13th here, not just for the sizeable water hazard that awaits, but for the 40-odd Nile crocodiles that lurk beneath the water. Go looking for errant balls entirely at your own risk.

Skukuza Golf Course (Kruger National Park, South Africa) – When you build a golf course where rhinos, elephants and buffalo prowl, and where the signs warn against running should you encounter one, you should probably expect a little danger. Keep a driver to hand at all times.

Carbrook Golf Club (Loganholme, Queensland, Australia) – The large lake lurking on the 15th at this course is not the real hazard here – it's the sharks beneath the surface you need to worry about. They found their way here after a local river burst its banks and never went home, surviving on a diet of golf balls and unwitting idiots.

La Jenny (Gironde, France) – The dress code at this course is refreshingly relaxed: you play naked, though shoes are probably permitted. It's Europe's one and so far only naturist course.

The Moon GC (Outer Space) – It may still be a few years off, but the plans are in place to create a course on the moon, tabled by forward-thinking Japanese company Shimizu Construction.

Top 10 greatest players in Rugby Union history*

1 **Jonah Lomu** (New Zealand) – Jonah was the world's first global rugby superstar and the way he dismantled England in the 1995 Rugby World Cup with four tries simply took the breath away. Freakish power and pace brought him 37 tries in only 63 Tests.

2 **Gareth Edwards** (Wales) – Despite hanging up his boots 35 years ago, Edwards is still revered as one of the finest players ever to grace the game. A live-wire scrum-half, his spine-tingling try for the 1973 Baa-Baas has more than three million views on YouTube.

3 **John Eales** (Australia) – You know a player is special when their nickname is 'Nobody', as in 'Nobody's perfect'. Eales had rare gifts; a goal-kicking lock, a phenomenal athlete and one of only seven men to lift the World Cup on two occasions – 1991 and 1999.

4 **Francois Pienaar** (South Africa) – The picture of Nelson Mandela handing the William Webb Ellis trophy to Springbok captain Francois Pienaar in 1995 reverberated around the world. It was a moment that united the Rainbow Nation, and Pienaar more than played his part.

5 **Richie McCaw** (New Zealand) – The first player to win 100 Tests, McCaw lifted the 2011 Rugby World Cup and led the All Blacks to the first unbeaten run in a calendar year since the game went professional. He's also, arguably, the best openside the world has ever seen.

6 **Brian O'Driscoll** (Ireland) – O'Driscoll is revered like no other in Ireland. Four Lions tours, a hat-trick of Heineken Cup victories and he looks likely to become the most capped player in international history; he doesn't need any longer introduction than BOD.

7 **Jonny Wilkinson** (England) – The embodiment of a sporting icon. Handsome, prodigiously gifted and modesty personified, he dropped the goal that helped England become the first Northern Hemisphere side to lift the World Cup, in 2003. An ambassador for the game who has transcended nationality.

8 **Sir Ian McGeechan** (Scotland) – A quick-thinking fly-half cum centre for Scotland, 'Geech' won 32 caps during the 1970s but is best recalled for doing more than any other individual to advance the Lions mythology during seven tours, as a player and coach.

9 **Willie John McBride** (Ireland) – Brought up in an era of acrimonious political divide, Ulsterman Willie John's achievements did more than most to unite Ireland. The lock's five Lions tours, including captaining in the victorious 1974 Springboks tour, will surely never be beaten.

10 **David Campese** (Australia) – Campese was a try-scoring phenomenon, with 64 tries in 101 Tests for the Wallabies between 1982 and 1996. A sublime finisher, he possessed blistering pace, allied to a sharp rugby brain and oodles of self-confidence. Often controversial, he remains one of the game's great characters.

*According to Owain Jones, the editor of *Rugby World*

Source: Owain Jones, *Rugby World*, www.rugbyworld.com; follow him @OwainJTJones

10 odd causes of sporting injuries

1 **Too much sex** – Pity poor Kevin Prince Boateng, the AC Milan footballer whose frequent injuries are apparently caused by his girlfriend, *Sports Illustrated* model Melissa Satta, demanding too much sex. Seven to ten times a week, apparently.

2 **A knife** – In 2001, the cerebrally challenged San Diego Padres pitcher Adam Eaton attempted to pierce the film on a DVD with a sharp knife – which slipped and stabbed him in the stomach. He didn't die, but it did end his season.

3 **Cologne** – When Spain's goalkeeper Santiago Cañizares knocked a bottle of cologne off his bathroom cabinet in 2002, his instincts kicked in. Attempting to control the bottle with his foot, the glass cut into the tendon in his big toe and ruled him out of that summer's World Cup.

4 **A red hot chilli pepper** – Former professional baseball infielder Bret Barberie was nixed after preparing himself a large mountain of jalapeño-heavy nachos. These he duly devoured, but then foolishly attempted to insert a contact lens without washing his hands. A burning eyeball kept him out of the next game.

5 **A very fast car** – Pint-sized Aston Villa defender Alan Wright was injured in the most Premier League of ways. Having just bought himself a nice new Ferrari, he strained his knee while reaching for the accelerator. The car was traded in soon after.

6 **An iron** – Golfer Bobby Cruickshank was injured in action on the 11th at Merion in the 1934 US Open. Leading by two, his approach came up short but hit a rock and popped on to the green. Cruickshank threw his club in the air in celebration, but forgot that gravity would have its way. Said club came crashing back down on his head and though he recovered, he ended up losing by two shots.

7 **A TV remote** – Having previously put his shoulder out while fishing, Manchester City goalkeeper David Seaman no doubt assumed watching TV would be a safer bet for a man of his advancing years. Not so – he ended up pulling a muscle as he reached for the remote control. Remarkably, fellow former Manchester City custodian David James injured himself in similar fashion.

8 **A dog** – Already sidelined with a broken finger at the start of the 2006/7 season, Aussie cricketer Matthew Hayden chose to keep his fitness levels up by going for a jog. Sadly, while out, he was attacked by a dog and bitten hard enough in the ankle to leave a 5 cm (2 in) gash.

9 **The sound of his own voice** – In a game against Birmingham City in 1975, Manchester United goalkeeper Alex Stepney dislocated his jaw by shouting loudly at his own defenders.

10 **A gun** – Having caught the game-winning touchdown in 2008's Super Bowl XLII, New York Giants wide receiver Plaxico Burress found global fame and a new five-year, $35 million contract. The money may have gone to his head, for in November that year, Burress accidentally shot himself in the leg (and, figuratively speaking, the foot) in a Manhattan nightclub with a gun he didn't have a permit to carry. He missed the rest of the season through injury and was sentenced to two years inside.

10 significant sporting bans

1 **Muhammad Ali: three and a half years (boxing)** – Refusing the
US military draft in 1967, Ali was banned for life and stripped
of his heavyweight title. The ban was later reduced and Ali reclaimed
his crown.

2 **Merle Hapes: eight years (American football)** – In 1946, the New
York Giants fullback was banned for life for informing the authorities
he had been asked to fix a game. Lifted eight years later, but he
never played again.

3 **David Layne, Peter Swan and Tony Kay: seven years (football)** –
Sheffield Wednesday footballers banned for betting on their own
team to lose in 1965. The ban was lifted seven years later.

4 **Billy Coutu: two and a half years (ice hockey)** – Banned for life for
battering one referee, attacking another and starting a mass brawl
playing for Boston Bruins in 1927, allegedly on the instruction of his
coach. Downgraded to two and a half years, but he never played
in the NHL again.

5 **Ron Artest: 86 games (basketball)** – Suspended for 86 games after
throwing punches at fans during the infamous 'Malice at the Palace'
brawl in 2004, Indiana Pacers' Ron Artest was reported to have
lost around $5 million in salary as a result. Ironically, he has since
changed his name to Metta World Peace.

6 **Latrell Sprewell: 68 games (basketball)** – Golden State shooting guard Sprewell was forced to sit out 68 games after attempting to choke his coach P. J. Carlesimo and dragging him to the ground during a training session.

7 **Billy Cook: 12 months (football)** – Oldham Athletic footballer banned for a year after refusing to leave the pitch after being sent off against Middlesbrough in 1915.

8 **Gilbert Arenas: 50 games (basketball)** – Suspended for most of the 2009/10 season for pulling a gun on a Washington Wizards team-mate in the locker room following an altercation over a reported gambling debt.

9 **Eric Cantona: nine months (football)** – Combustible Manchester United striker banned for nine months for kung-fu kicking a Crystal Palace fan in 1995. A two-week prison sentence was overturned on appeal, Cantona doing 120 hours community service instead.

10 **Frank Barson: six months (football)** – Watford footballer banned in 1928 for allegedly kicking an opponent, an accusation refuted by both Barson and the opponents. A 5,000-signature petition was presented to the FA in his defence, to no avail.

10 terrible sporting 'chokes'

① **Greg Norman: The Masters, Augusta** (1996) – Six shots ahead going into the final round of the 1996 Masters, the Great White Shark somehow turned it into a five-shot deficit as Nick Faldo reeled him in and spat him out. A choke of truly epic proportions.

② **Scott Boswell: Cheltenham & Gloucester Trophy final** (2001) – Impressive in the semi-final, Leicestershire's Boswell capitulated remarkably in the final, bowling two overs for 23. Not in itself remarkable, only they consisted of nine wides, eight alone in the second over and five of them in a row. Considered to be one of the worst overs in cricket history.

③ **Jana Novotna: Wimbledon final** (1993) – Leading Steffi Graf 6-7, 6-1 4-1 and 40-30 in the sixth game of the deciding set, Novotna had a service point for 5-1. Cue a double fault and the greatest capitulation in a Wimbledon final. Ten minutes later Graf had won and Novotna was crying on the Duchess of Kent's shoulder.

④ **David Bedford: Olympic 5,000 metre final** (1972) – Despite underperforming in the 10,000 metres, such was Bedford's reputation that swift redemption was expected in the 5,000. It seemed to be panning out that way as the Brit found himself nicely placed after four laps, before the demons of self-doubt crept in and he dropped woefully down the field.

⑤ **Deportivo La Coruña: La Liga** (1993/4) – Back in the days before Barcelona and Real Madrid won everything, Deportivo had the La Liga title in their hands, or at their feet. Against Valencia, they had a penalty kick in injury time that would secure the title at the expense of Barcelona. Up stepped Miroslav Djukic for his shot at immortality – and rolled his woeful attempt into the arms of José Gonzalez. The rest is history.

Jean Van de Velde: Open Championship (1999) – Heading down the final hole with a seemingly unassailable three-shot lead, the Frenchman seemed set to pull off an unexpected victory, providing he played it safe. Instead, he bounced his ball all over the shop like a first-timer and scraped into a play-off, which he lost.

Jimmy White: World snooker final (1994) – Finally, after five previous final defeats, 'the Whirlwind' was within sight of snooker's greatest prize. At 17-17 with Stephen Hendry in the deciding frame, a simple black off the spot would as good as win it for him – he missed by a mile and handed it to Hendry on a silver plate.

Gavin Hastings: Rugby World Cup (1991) – There's no such thing as a routine kick in front of the posts in a World Cup semi-final against England, as the ordinarily ice-cool Gavin Hastings proved. Shanking it hopelessly wide, England applied additional salt by edging it thanks to a Rob Andrew drop goal.

Anthony Fleet: BDO World Championships (2010) – Australian darts 'star' Anthony Fleet is infamous for imploding against Martin 'Wolfy' Adams. Dropping his darts like a nervous novice, he then threw 26, 41, 60, 60, 5, 41, 22, 80 and 11 in the first leg en route to a swift, sobering defeat. 'I have embarrassed myself,' he later reflected.

England's penalty takers: repeatedly (Turin 1990, Wembley 1996, St Etienne 1998, Gelsenkirchen 2006...) – Heroic for 120 minutes, plus stoppage time, pathetic from 12 yards when it inevitably goes to penalty kicks. Pearce, Waddle, Southgate, Ince, Batty, Lampard, Gerrard, Carragher – the names may change but never the outcome.

10 greatest comebacks in sporting history

1 **Henri Cochet: Wimbledon semi-final** (1927) – A Wimbledon semi-finalist in 1927, Frenchman Cochet found himself two sets and 5-1 down to the American 'Big Bill' Tiden in the fifth. Overpowered, *oui*, but overwhelmed, *non*. Cochet began taking the ball earlier and produced a miracle: 2-6, 4-6, 7-5, 6-4, 6-3.

2 **Europe: vs. USA, Ryder Cup** (2012) – Thirteen years after the USA overturned a record 6-10 deficit on the final day, an Ian Poulter-powered Europe fought back from the same deficit in the 'Miracle of Medinah' to win eight and tie one of the Sunday singles and somehow, inexplicably prevail 14½ to 13½.

3 **Lasse Viren: Olympics 10,000 metre final** (1972) – Falling at the halfway stage, few would have expected Finnish policeman Viren to complete the race, let alone clamber back to his feet and tirelessly chase down Britain's David Bedford to take gold. Only Viren himself perhaps, who did so in a World Record time.

4 **Liverpool: vs. AC Milan, Champions League final** (2005) – Three down and seemingly dead and buried by half-time, a Steven Gerrard header after 54 minutes turned the 2005 Champions League final on its head. Liverpool scored three times in six minutes to draw level then prevailed on penalties.

5 **Red Rum: Grand National** (1973) – Thirty lengths from home, Grand National favourite and one of horse racing's finest ever nags, the Australian Crisp, appeared home and hosed. Until Red Rum, carrying 10.4 kg (23 lb) less, romped past to win on the line and announce his arrival to the world.

6 **Charlton Athletic: vs. Huddersfield Town, Division Two** (1957) – Trailing Bill Shankly's Huddersfield 5-1 and down to ten men with just 28 minutes remaining, Charlton's Johnny Summers had clearly not read the script – he scored five times to draw the score level at 6-6, then set up John Ryan to win the match with the final kick of a glorious game.

Hampshire: vs. Warwickshire, County Championship (1922) – More incredible even than Ian Botham's Ashes heroics in 1981, here Hampshire found themselves bowled out for 15 and following on, still a hopeless 208 runs shy. Unperturbed, they set about making 521, then bowled their opponents out for 158 to steal cricket's most unlikely victory.

Dennis Taylor: vs. Steve Davis, World Championship final (1985) – After losing the first seven frames against world champion Steve Davis, the Irishman with the upside down glasses was in danger of being swept away. But when the metronomic Davis made his first mistake, the fightback began. It went to 17-all and deep into the night – Taylor won it on the final, re-spotted black.

Muhammad Ali: vs. George Foreman, WBC/WBA Heavyweight Championship (1974) – Aged 32 and clearly on the wane, Ali entered the 'Rumble in the Jungle' against a world champion six years younger and unbeaten in 40 fights. Employing the rope-a-dope tactic of resting on the ropes, Ali cleverly let Foreman blow himself out before knocking him down and out in the eighth.

Buffalo Bills: vs. Houston Oilers, NFL playoffs (1993) – The greatest comeback in NFL history, the Bills found themselves 32 down in the third quarter and relying on backup quarterback Frank Reich to be the hero. His four touchdown passes pulled the game back to 35-35 and took it into overtime, where a 29 m (32 yd) field goal stole a ridiculous victory.

10 remarkable unbeaten runs

1 **Byron Nelson** – The golfer secured 11 consecutive PGA Tour wins in 1945, including the PGA Championship.

2 **Jerry Rice** – In American football, the NFL Oakland Raider's wide receiver went 274 consecutive games with a reception (making a catch), a run lasting from 1985 to 2004.

3 **Wayne Gretzky** – The NHL ice hockey player scored at least one point in 51 consecutive games for the Edmonton Oilers between 1983 and 1984.

4 **Julio César Chávez** – The Mexican boxer won his first 87 bouts, the longest winning streak in boxing, in any weight class. The 88th bout was drawn; his first defeat came in his 90th fight.

5 **Cal Ripken** – Between 1982 and 1998, Ripken clocked up 2,632 consecutive games played for baseball's Baltimore Orioles.

6 **Martina Navratilova –** The Czech recorded 74 consecutive wins in women's singles tennis in 1984, which saw her win 13 consecutive tournaments. Only injury forced that run to an end.

7 **Joe DiMaggio** – In 1941, the New York Yankees star set a record with a 56-game hitting streak – baseball games in which a player gets at least one base hit.

8 **Drew Brees** – The New Orleans Saints quarterback holds the record for the most consecutive American football games (54) with at least one touchdown pass, recorded in 2012.

9 **Edwin Moses** – Between 1978 and 1987, this track and field star won 122 straight races in the 400 metre hurdles.

10 **Arsène Wenger** – The Frenchman managed Arsenal to a 49-game unbeaten run, stretching between May 2003 and October 2004, a run which ended in a controversial defeat at Manchester United.

Source: Real Clear Sports, www.realclearsports.com

0 curious collective names for animals

- A cauldron of bats

- A business of ferrets

- A bloat of hippopotamuses

- A conspiracy of lemurs

- A parliament of owls

- An unkindness of ravens

- An army of frogs

- A consortium of crabs

- A quiver of cobras

- A pandemonium of parrots

ANIMALS, CREATURES & BEASTIES

10 running speeds of animals relative to the world's fastest man

ANIMALS, CREATURES & BEASTIES

ANIMAL	TOP SPEED
❶ Cheetah	116 km/h (72 mph)
❷ Pronghorn antelope	98 km/h (61 mph)
❸ African lion	88 km/h (55 mph)
❹ Greyhound	69 km/h (43 mph)
❺ Domestic cat	48 km/h (30 mph)
❻ Human (Usain Bolt)	43 km/h (27 mph)
❼ Elephant	40 km/h (25 mph)
❽ Squirrel	19 km/h (12 mph)
❾ Mouse	13 km/h (8 mph)
❿ Garden snail	0.05 km/h (0.03 mph)

Source: Compiled by Dr Leon Foster for the Centre for Sports Engineering Research, Sheffield Hallam University; Engineering Sport, www.engineeringsport.co.uk

0 lesser known dangerous dogs

- **Chow Chow** – Aka Songshi Quan or 'puffy lion dog', a cuddly looking but extremely aggressive dog. Its human kills are close to double figures.

- **Tosa Inu** – Large, muscular Japanese dog with powerful jaws and a fierce sense of loyalty to its owner. Originally bred for fighting. Banned in the UK.

- **Fila Brasileiro** – Aka the Brazilian mastiff, a dog bred for tracking but with an aggressive, unpredictable nature. Banned in the UK.

- **Dogo Argentino** – Large, white, muscular dog developed in Argentina for big-game hunting. Banned in the UK and parts of the USA.

- **Boerboel** – Large, powerful mastiff of South African origin, bred for security and game hunting. Loyal and protective.

- **Bully Kuta** – Aka the Pakistani mastiff, a large, muscular canine and another dog bred originally for hunting and guarding.

- **Cane Corso** – Italian molosser, a distant relative of the Neapolitan mastiff, a hound bred for catching cattle and swine.

- **Perro de Presa Canario** – Large Canary Islands dog, bred for working livestock, with aggressive tendencies that have seen them kill at least four humans.

- **Caucasian Oucharka** – Aka the Caucasian shepherd dog, bred to protect livestock and with fierce tendencies. Dangerously courageous.

- **American Bandogge** – Ferociously powerful pit bull terrier–Neapolitan mastiff crossbreed, and justifiably referred to as 'an intruder's worst nightmare'.

Not all of the dogs on this list are instinctively dangerous but the breeds have a history of aggressive and often unpredictable behaviour. All should be approached with caution.

10 dangerous sea creatures (that aren't sharks)

1 **Cone snail** (Indo-Pacific) – It may look to be a pretty shell sat on the bottom of the ocean, but this little beast will shoot its toxin into you using a clever harpoon. Unless treated quickly, a swift and painful death can often follow.

2 **Box jellyfish** (Indo-Pacific) – Gelatinous killer boasting dozens of tentacles packed full of poisonous toxins that can – and do – kill humans in minutes.

3 **Portuguese man-of-war** (Indo-Pacific) – Less deadly than the box jellyfish, though the man-of-war has killed. Those who've survived say its sting feels as painful as death.

4 **Stingray** (coastal tropical and subtropical marine waters globally) – Though they rarely attack humans, the tail packs venom that can cause great pain and, on occasion, a horrific death.

5 **Stonefish** (Indo-Pacific, Caribbean) – The most venomous fish in the world looks like an ordinary rock but shoots out deadly venom should you inadvertently stand on it.

6 **Pufferfish** (South-east Asia) – More likely to kill you if you eat it (see fugu, page 116), but there is no antidote to a bite, which paralyzes the diaphragm, causing suffocation.

7 **Banded sea krait** (Indo-Pacific) – Although far too timid to usually bother humans, this sea-dwelling serpent packs a venom ten times as toxic as a rattlesnake's.

8 **Striped eel catfish** (Indo-Pacific) – Armed with venomous spines capable of delivering a highly painful sting. It's rarely fatal to humans, though deaths have been reported.

9 **Blue-ringed octopus** (Indo-Pacific) – The poison packed in this tiny cephalopod's neurotoxins can kill a human in minutes. There is no known anti-venom. Lurks in tide pools.

10 **Pfeffer's flamboyant cuttlefish** (Indo-Pacific) – Photogenic little mollusc that is every bit as deadly as the blue-ringed octopus. Rarely stings humans, but that doesn't mean it won't if you go bothering it.

Top 10 most common birds in the UK

BIRD	ESTIMATED NUMBER OF TERRITORIES*
Wren	8.6 million
Robin	6.7 million
Chaffinch	6.2 million
Woodpigeon	5.4 million
House sparrow	5.3 million
Blackbird	5.1 million
Blue tit	3.6 million
Great tit	2.6 million
Dunnock	2.5 million
Willow warbler	2.4 million

*Territories in which each type of bird was counted, 2009; latest available figures

Source: The Royal Society for the Protection of Birds, www.rspb.org.uk; information via www.researchgate.net

ANIMALS, CREATURES & BEASTIES

Top 10 most dangerous snakes in the world

SNAKE/LOCATION	SCORES*	TOTAL SCOR

❶ Puff adder (*Bitis arietans*) (Africa) — 3/4/3/4/4/5 — 2
It's said that 100 mg of its venom can kill a healthy adult human male – its typical venom yield is between 100 and 350 mg.

❷ Barba amarilla (*Bothrops asper*) — 4/4/2/4/5/4 — 2
(Central/South America)
Large, aggressive snakes possessing significant quantities of a high toxic venom that is necrotizing and frequently fatal.

❸ Papuan taipan — 4/3/5/3/5/3 — 2
(*Oxyuranus scutellatus canni*) (New Guinea)
A single bite, with envenomation, can result in death within 30 minutes.

❹ Coastal taipan (*Oxyuranus scutellatus*) — 4/3/5/3/5/2 — 2
(Australia)
Producer of the most toxic venom of any snake in the world, a sing bite contains enough venom to kill 100 full grown men, or 12,000 guinea pigs.

❺ Russell's viper (*Daboia russelii*) (Asia) — 3/3/3/3/4/5 — 2
Its venom results in falling blood pressure, reduced heart rate, bloo clotting and, if the anti-venom is not forthcoming, imminent death.

❻ Common lancehead (*Bothrops atrox*) — 3/3/2/4/5/4 — 2
(Central/South America)
Its venom consists mostly of fast-acting and lethal hemotoxins, causing nausea, blackouts, paralysis and, if untreated, death.

❼ King cobra (*Ophiophagus hannah*) (Asia) — 5/5/3/3/3/2 — 2
Shy but aggressive when cornered, a single bite can possess enoug neurotoxin to kill 20 people.

SNAKE/LOCATION	SCORES*	TOTAL SCORE†

Black mamba (*Dendroaspis polylepis*) 4/3/3/2/5/3 20
(Africa)
Fast, aggressive and deadly – its bite packs enough venom to kill an elephant. It usually delivers around 120 mg: just 10–15 mg will kill a human.

Saw-scaled viper (*Echis carinatus*) 1/1/5/2/5/5 19
(Africa and Asia)
A highly venomous snake that will bite if it feels threatened, frequently with fatal results. Nocturnal, it also likes to conceal itself in sand.

Mexican West Coast rattlesnake 3/4/2/4/3/3 19
(*Crotalus basiliscus*) (Central/South America)
Large, heavy-bodied snake possessing huge amounts of highly toxic venom, long fangs and a dangerous temperament.

*Scores are given for, in order, average size/venom yield/venom toxicity/fang length/disposition-attitude/bites per year and are marked low (1) to high (5). Figures are based on 'historical averages and other data sets'. Because not all snakebites are recorded, exact figures do not exist

†Where total score is equal, snakes are ranked by number of bites per year

Source: The Black Hills Reptile Gardens, www.reptilegardens.com

Black Hills Reptile Gardens is a reptile zoo in South Dakota, USA, which maintains the largest and most diverse collection of venomous snakes found in captivity.

10 curious creatures of Greek mythology

1 **Typhon** – Part man, part preposterous winged and feathered beast with legs made of giant, hissing snakes. His eyes flashed fire and from his arms sprang a hundred heads of a fierce dragon with black tongues.

2 **Satyr** – The upper body of a muscular man, the lower bits of a goat. Satyrs resided in woods and mountains or accompanied the Greek god of wine Dionysus on his journeys, dancing around joyfully with the nymphs and drinking.

3 **Hecatonchires** – Three gruesome offspring of Gaia and Ouranos: Briareus (the Vigorous), Cottus (the Furious) and Gyes (the Big-limbed), each baring hundreds of arms and 50 heads, and each built for battle.

4 **Centaur** – Boasting the upper body of a man and the lower region of a horse, centaurs were, in the main, aggressive, drunken creatures.

5 **Minotaur** – A cannibalistic monster with the body of a man and the head of a bull. Minotaur was created by Pasiphaë, the wife of King Minos, when she mated with a bull that was sent to her by the god Poseidon. As you do.

Graeae – Three sisters named Enyo (the Shocking), Pemphredo (the Horrifying) and Deino (the Dreadful), who had taken the form of rancid old crones since birth. They shared a single eye and a single tooth, which they took turns using.

Manticore – Similar in style to the Egyptian sphinx, a manticore had the body of a lion, a human head with three rows of sharp teeth and a voice like a trumpet. Some were horned, some winged, and some both, with the tail of a dragon or a scorpion that fired poison from its spines to paralyze its victim, which it would eat whole.

Chimera – A beastly creature with the body of a lion, the fire-breathing head of a goat and the tail of a snake.

Cerberus – A devilish 'hellhound' from both Greek and Roman mythology, Cerberus guarded the gates of the underworld and boasted three snarling heads – or as many as a hundred, according to some theories.

Harpy – A female creature with the body of a muscular turkey and the head of a woman, with bronze wings, sharp claws and long, flowing hair. Notorious for its speed, its greed and its obnoxious smells.

10 interesting facts about dinosaurs

1 **The first named dinosaur was Megalosaurus** – Named in 1824 by Reverend William Buckland, its name meaning 'great lizard'. It was about 9 m (29.5 ft) long and 3 m (10 ft) tall.

2 **The most intelligent was Troodon** – A hunting dinosaur, about 2 m (6.5 ft) long, Troodon had a brain size similar to that of a mammal or bird of today. Blessed with stereoscopic vision and grasping hands.

3 **The stupidest were sauropodomorphs** – Although Stegosaurus had a brain the size of a walnut, about 3 cm (1.2 in) long and weighing 75 g (2.6 oz), if comparing brain size to body size, sauropodomorphs, such as Plateosaurus, were perhaps the dumbest dinosaurs of all.

4 **Sauroposeidon was the tallest** – The Brachiosaurid group of sauropods had front legs longer than its rear legs, giving them a giraffe-like stance. Brachiosaurus – the best known of the group – was 13 m (43 ft) tall, but Sauroposeidon was the tallest, growing to around 18.5 m (60 ft).

5 **The smallest was Lesothosaurus** – The smallest, fully grown fossil dinosaur found is this little bird-hipped plant-eater, which was about the size of a chicken. Smaller fossilized examples have been found but have only been baby dinosaurs.

Seismosaurus was the longest – Measuring more than 40 m (130 ft), which is roughly as long as five double-decker buses, it was related to the better known Diplodocus, which for a long time held the honour.

The fastest-running were ornithomimids – The speediest dinosaurs were the ostrich-mimic ornithomimids, such as Dromiceiomimus, which are thought to have been able to run at speeds of up to 60 km/h (37 mph).

The oldest dinosaurs have been found in Madagascar – The oldest known dinosaurs lived 230 million years ago in Madagascar. As yet they have not been formally named. Before this, Eoraptor held the title at 228 million years.

The longest dinosaur name is Micropachycephalosaurus – The name means 'tiny, thick-headed lizard'. Its fossils have been found in China, and it was named in 1978 by the Chinese palaeontologist Dong.

The fiercest was Utahraptor – Although Tyrannosaurus rex looked the most ferocious, in terms of overall cunning, determination and its array of vicious weapons, Utahraptor was the most fierce. It measured 7 m (23 ft), and was a very powerful, agile and intelligent predator.

Source: The Dinosaur Museum, www.thedinosaurmuseum.com

10 most borrowed library books in the UK*

1 *The Story of Tracy Beaker* (2002), Jacqueline Wilson
– Most borrowed book

2 *The Thursday Friend* (1999), Catherine Cookson
– Most borrowed adult fiction book

3 **Charles Dickens** – Most borrowed pre-20th-century classic author

4 *How to Cook, Book One* (1998), Delia Smith
– Most borrowed cookery book

5 *A Child Called It* (1995), Dave Pelzer – Most borrowed biography

6 *Down Under* (2000), Bill Bryson – Most borrowed travel book

7 *Berlin: The Downfall, 1945* (2002), Antony Beevor
– Most borrowed history book

8 *Taking on the World* (2010), Ellen MacArthur
– Most borrowed book on sports and outdoor pursuits

9 *Revolting Rhymes* (1982), Roald Dahl, illustrated by Quentin Blake
– Most borrowed children's poetry book

10 *Where's Wally?* (1987), Martin Handford
– Most borrowed children's picture book

*For the period 2000–2010

Source: The Public Lending Right, www.plr.uk.com

Top 10 largest book advances of all time*

ESTIMATED ADVANCE	TITLE/YEAR	AUTHOR
$15 million	*My Life* (2004)	Bill Clinton
$14 million	For a future book (due Jun 2014)	Hillary Clinton
$8.75 million	*In My Own Words* (1994)	Pope John Paul II
$8.5 million	*The Age of Turbulence* (2008)	Alan Greenspan
$8 million	*Living History* (2003)	Hillary Clinton
$8 million	*The Casual Vacancy* (2012)	J. K. Rowling
$7.7 million	*Life* (2011)	Keith Richards
$7.1 million	*Straight from the Gut* (2001)	Jack Welch
$7 million	*Seinlanguage* (1994)	Jerry Seinfeld
$7 million	*Decision Points* (2010)	George W. Bush

*Reported figures as at October 2013, for with book advances, we'll never truly know

BOOKS & NEWSPAPERS

10 weird book titles

1 *Cooking With Poo* (2011) – Saiyuud Diwong

2 *Mr Andoh's Pennine Diary: Memoirs of a Japanese Chicken Sexer in 1935 Hebden Bridge* (2011) – Stephen Curry and Takayoshi Andoh

3 *The Great Singapore Penis Panic and the Future of American Mass Hysteria* (2011) – Scott D. Mendelson

4 *The Mushroom in Christian Art* (2011) – John A. Rush

5 *Collectible Spoons of the Third Reich* (2009) – James A. Yannes

6 *I Was Tortured by the Pygmy Love Queen* (2007) – Jasper McCutcheon

7 *Greek Rural Postmen and Their Cancellation Numbers* (1994) – edited by Derek Willan

8 *People Who Don't Know They're Dead: How They Attach Themselves to Unsuspecting Bystanders and What to Do About It* (2005) – Gary Leon Hill

9 *The Big Book of Lesbian Horse Stories* (2003) – Alisa Surkis and Monica Nolan

10 *Last Chance at Love: Terminal Romances* (1981) – Various authors

Source: *The Bookseller*, www.thebookseller.com

0 more weird book titles

The Book of Marmalade: Its Antecedents, Its History, and Its Role in the World Today (1986) - Anne Wilson

How to Shit in the Woods: An Environmentally Sound Approach to a Lost Art (1989) - Kathleen Meyer

Lesbian Sadomasochism Safety Manual (1995) - Pat Califa

How to Avoid Huge Ships (1982) - John W. Trimmer

Managing a Dental Practice: The Genghis Khan Way (2010) - Michael R. Young

Weeds in a Changing World: British Crop Protection Council Symposium Proceedings No. 64 (1999) - Charles H. Stirton

Highlights in the History of Concrete (1994) - C. C. Stanley

Crocheting Adventures with Hyperbolic Planes (2009) - Daina Taimina

The Madam as Entrepreneur: Career Management in House Prostitution (1979) - Barbara Sherman Heyl

Proceedings of the Second International Workshop on Nude Mice (1978) - Various authors

Source: *The Bookseller*, www.thebookseller.com

10 great opening lines of literary classics

1 '**Marley was dead, to begin with.**' – *A Christmas Carol* (1843), Charles Dickens

2 '**In the beginning God created the heavens and the earth.**' – The Bible, various contributors

3 '**Mr. and Mrs. Dursley, of number four, Privet Drive, were proud to say that they were perfectly normal, thank you very much.**' – *Harry Potter and the Philosopher's Stone* (1997), J. K. Rowling

4 '**It was a bright cold day in April, and the clocks were striking thirteen.**' – *Nineteen Eighty-Four* (1949), George Orwell

5 '**When a day that you happen to know is Wednesday starts off by sounding like Sunday, there is something seriously wrong somewhere.**' – *The Day of the Triffids* (1951), John Wyndham

6 '**The sweat wis lashing oafay Sick Boy; he wis trembling.**' – *Trainspotting* (1993), Irvine Welsh

7 '**Amerigo Bonasera sat in New York Criminal Court Number 3 and waited for justice; vengeance on the men who had so cruelly hurt his daughter, who had tried to dishonor her.**' – *The Godfather* (1969), Mario Puzo

8 '**We go about our daily lives understanding almost nothing about the world.**' (From the Introduction by Carl Sagan) – *A Brief History of Time* (1988), Stephen Hawking

9 '**These two very old people are the father and mother of Mr. Bucket.**' – *Charlie and the Chocolate Factory* (1964), Roald Dahl

10 '**FIRST EVENING: INDOORS. Address the boys on "Scoutcraft", giving a summary of the whole scheme, as in this chapter, with demonstrations or lantern slides, etc. Swear in the scouts, form Patrols, and give shoulder knots.**' – *Scouting for Boys: A Handbook for Instruction in Good Citizenship* (1908), Robert Baden-Powell

0 great newspaper headlines

- **Man Stole Tortoise to Pay for Booze** – *Hartlepool Mail*

- **Kitten That Looks Like Hitler – Pictures** – *Cambridge Evening News*

- **Oven Removed From Home** – *Isle of Wight County Gazette*

- **King's Lynn Woman Reunited with Lost Hat She Mislaid on Bus Ride in Felixstowe After Suffolk Police Appeal** – *Eastern Daily Press*

- **Toy Shop Owner Throws a Tantrum** – *Bishop's Stortford Advertiser*

- **Large Lorry Negotiates Tight Bend in North Walsham** – *Norwich Evening News*

- **Rotten Tree Falls in Garden** – *Hornsey, Crouch End and Muswell Hill Journal*

- **'I'm Not Dead' Says Gran** – *Kent Messenger*

- **OAP Baffles Experts with His 2ft Long Courgettes** – *South London Press*

- **'Semi-erect' OAP Caught Shampooing His Genitals on a Bus Claims He's 'No Hardened Criminal'** – *Bedfordshire on Sunday*

 BOOKS & NEWSPAPERS

10 memorable *Sunday Sport* headlines

1. Statue of Elvis Found on Mars

2. Gazza's Face Grows on White Cliffs of Dover

3. World War 2's Best-Kept Secret: Adolf Hitler was a Woman

4. 3 Inch Dog Ate My Missus

5. Hide & Seek Champ Found Dead in Cupboard

6. World's Ugliest Woman Dies After Look in Mirror

7. Monkey Lands Plane

8. Drunk Cat Burns Down Chippy

9. Gordon Ramsay Sex Dwarf Eaten by Badger

10. Man Fights Shark with Wife's False Teeth

Source: *Sunday Sport*, www.sundaysport.com and tweeting at @thesundaysport

10 words that will make you sound more intelligent

1. **Abligurition** (*ab-li-gur-i-tion*) – Spending excessive amounts of money on food

2. **Callipygian** (*cal-lipy-gian*) – Possessing shapely buttocks

3. **Bablatrice** (*bab-la-trice*) – An overly talkative woman

4. **Nudiustertian** (*nudi-uster-tian*) – Pertaining to the day before yesterday

5. **Obambulate** (*ob-am-bu-late*) – To wander aimlessly

6. **Impecunious** (*imp-ec-unious*) – Being penniless, lacking money

7. **Anililagnia** (*an-il-il-ag-nia*) – An attraction to older women

8. **Philopolemical** (*phil-o-polemic-al*) – Being fond of controversy or arguments

9. **Gambrinous** (*gam-brinous*) – Being full of beer and most likely drunken

10. **Furciferous** (*fur-cif-er-ous*) – Rascally or roguish

10 common phrases we've borrowed from abroad

1 **Angst** – Borrowed from the Germans, a word meaning a deep-rooted fear or dread, generally referring to the state of the world.

2 **Carte blanche** – Taken from the French, literally translating as 'blank paper' and referring to the freedom to act as you choose.

3 **De rigueur** – Another French classic, meaning socially required or obligatory.

4 **Dolce vita** – Usually written or spoken as 'la dolce vita', translating literally as 'the sweet life', referring to a life of great opulence.

5 **Doppelgänger** – Meaning an apparition or double of a living person, taken from mid-19th-century German, literally translated as 'double-goer'.

6 **Fait accompli** – Meaning, in French, an accomplished fact, and generally one that cannot be reversed so must be accepted.

7 **Schadenfreude** – A German word fusing *Schaden* (harm) and *Freude* (joy) to form a word relating to the joy derived from the misfortune of another or others.

8 **Smorgasbord** – Borrowed from the Swedes, often referring to an impressive range of open sandwiches but more generally used when you're offered a wide variety of something or other.

9 **Faux pas** – In French, meaning literally 'false step'. We've taken it to refer to those occasions when a person blurts out a particularly tactless remark in the company of others.

10 **Zeitgeist** – The Germans created this by forging *Zeit* (time) and *Geist* (spirit), the result being a word that refers to the spirit of a particular period of time or generation.

10 Latin phrases we've taken as our own

1 **Ad hoc** – Translating as 'for this' and generally signifying a specific solution for a specific problem, and one that is nontransferable to any other tasks.

2 **Ad nauseam** – Meaning to do something to a ridiculous extent; literally, to the point of nausea.

3 **Bona fide** – Meaning, literally, 'in good faith'. 'A bona fide painting of the *Mona Lisa*', for example.

4 **In loco parentis** – Meaning 'in the place of a parent'; for example, 'the teacher was used to acting *in loco parentis*'.

5 **Mea culpa** – Literally translated as 'through my own fault', as in 'I am culpable and deserve to be punished'. For example, 'the politician's *mea culpa* was appeasing no one'.

6 **Non sequitur** – Meaning a comment or claim that is unrelated to what has gone before, *sequitur* translating as 'the conclusion of an inference'.

7 **Postmortem** – *Post* meaning 'after', *mortem* meaning 'death', most commonly the practice of inspecting a body following death. (Ante-mortem means 'preceding death'.)

8 **Quid pro quo** – Translating as 'something for something', when exchanging items of a similar value. Most commonly associated with an underhand trade – 'you scratch my back and I'll scratch yours'.

9 **Vice versa** – Indicating that something can be reversed or taken to be the other way round, from *vicis*, meaning 'change' and *vertere*, meaning 'to turn'.

10 **Et cetera** – A combination of 'and' (*et*) and 'the rest' (*cetera*), bolted on to the end of a sentence and meaning the stuff we can't be bothered to mention.

10 commonly used slang terms for money

1 **Bin: £1** – Bin lid, rhymes with quid. 'Quid' is thought to be from the Latin *quid pro quo*, meaning something for something, an exchange (see page 215). Others prefer 'nicker', possibly connected to the nickel used in the minting of coins or to the American slang use of 'nickel' for a $5 note (rather than the usual 5 cents), which in the late 1800s was valued close enough to £1 to carry some weight.

2 **Godiva: £5** – Lady Godiva, rhymes with fiver.

3 **Cock: £10** – Cock and hen, rhymes with ten.

4 **Commodore: £15** – Three times a Lady (Godiva), so £15. 'Once, twice, three times a lady' was a lyric made famous by Lionel Richie's Commodores.

5 **Score: £20** – Reportedly from the Old Norse *skor*, meaning a notch on a stick used for counting (some say sheep). People often counted in 20s, with every 20th notch scored larger.

6 **Pony: £25** – Theories abound but 'to pony up' has meant 'to pay up' in American slang since 1824. Some suggest the figure of £25 relates to the price paid for a small horse at the time, though this is at best speculation.

Bull's-eye: £50 – The score when hitting the bull's-eye in the centre of the dartboard. £50 can also be called 'half a ton' (see No. 8).

Ton: £100 – The most plausible reason being that a ton (when referring to cargo capacity) is a measurement of 100 cubic feet. Applied to anything where 100 is involved, be it speed, age or runs in cricket.

Monkey: £500 – Most likely a reference to the 500 rupee note, which featured a monkey on it, the term coined by British soldiers returning home from India in the early 1900s.

Rio: £1,000 – From the days when £1,000 was a more significant amount of money than it is today, 'grand' (meaning very large) became its common slang term. This later became 'Rio' – a reference to the large and impressive Rio Grande river. Some also claim it refers to the footballer Rio Ferdinand, although that makes less sense.

Because there is no definitive list of slang derivations, these represent the most plausible reasons for the names often used.

10 everyday phrases with macabre origins

LANGUAGES

1 **Pay through the nose** – From the 9th-century poll tax imposed by Vikings: they slit the noses from tip to eyebrow of anyone who refused to pay the tax.

2 **Gone to pot** – Various theories exist but the most sinister refers to a time when boiling to death was still a legal punishment.

3 **Deadline** – A line literally drawn to prevent prisoners escaping during the American Civil War. If they crossed it, they were shot dead.

4 **Saved by the bell** – For a short time after burial, if the 'dead' person wasn't actually dead, he'd pull a string around his wrist that rang a bell above ground.

5 **Pressed for an answer** – Dates back to the Middle Ages, when heavy weights were placed on the chest of a suspect to press a confession out of them.

6 **Hoist by your own petard** – A petard was a 16th-century French bomb so unreliable that it would often blow up the unfortunate man planting it.

7 **Hauled over the coals** – In the Middle Ages, suspected witches were hauled over hot coals. If they survived, they were innocent.

8 **Diehard** – Dating back to the 1700s, this term referred to men who struggled the longest when they were hanged.

9 **Bite the bullet** – Before the arrival of anaesthetic, soldiers endured operations by clenching a bullet between their teeth to numb the pain.

10 **Rule of thumb** – In 1886, judge Sir Francis Buller ruled 'a man was entitled to beat his wife with a stick, provided it was no thicker than his thumb'.

Source: Genes Reunited, www.genesreunited.co.uk

10 very usable Shakespearean insults

1 **'You are not worth another word, else I'd call you knave'**
– *All's Well That Ends Well*

2 **'Thou art unfit for any place but hell'** – *Richard III*

3 **'Thou art like a toad; ugly and venomous'** – *As You Like It*

4 **'I do desire we may be better strangers'** – *As You Like It*

5 **'Your brain is as dry as the remainder biscuit after voyage'**
– *As You Like It*

6 **'I scorn you, scurvy companion'** – *Henry IV, Part 2*

7 **'Dissembling harlot, thou art false in all!'** – *The Comedy of Errors*

8 **'More of your conversation would infect my brain'** – *Coriolanus*

9 **'Thou mis-shapen dick!'** – *Henry VI, Part 3*

10 **'Thou art as fat as butter'** – *Henry IV, Part 1*

10 ways to say 'I love you' in a foreign language

1 *Je t'aime* (*je tame*) – French

2 *Te amo/Ti amo* (*tee-armo*) – Spanish/Italian

3 *Ich liebe dich* (*ick leeb-eh dick*) – German

4 *Aishite imasu* (*aye-shyte ima-su*) – Japanese

5 *Ik hou van je* (*ik hoo van yay*) – Dutch

6 *Eu te amo* (*yu tee armo*) – Portuguese

7 *Phom rak khun* (*fom rack koon*) – Thai

8 *Kocham Cię* (*ko-sham cee*) – Polish

9 *Ya tebya lyublyu* (*ya teb-ya lou-blue*) – Russian

10 *Jag älskar dig* (*yag alsk-ar dig*) – Swedish

Top 10 most educated countries in the world

COUNTRY	PERCENTAGE OF ADULT POPULATION WITH A TERTIARY (COLLEGE) DEGREE*
1 **Russian Federation**	53.5
2 **Canada**	51.3
3 **Japan**	46.4
3 **Israel**	46.4
5 **USA**	42.5
6 **Korea**	40.4
7 **United Kingdom**	39.4
8 **New Zealand**	39.3
8 **Finland**	39.3
10 **Australia**	38.3

*2010–11 figures

**Source: Organization for Economic Co-operation and Development,
www.oecd.org**

10 common grammar mistakes

1 **Acute** and **chronic** – 'Acute' means sharp, as in an illness or a situation that rapidly worsens. 'Chronic' may be every bit as painful but it's more likely to be longer lasting than to rapidly deteriorate.

2 **Affect** and **effect** – There are exceptions here but the basic rule is that 'affect' means to influence something in some way. An effect is the result of something occurring. You can *affect* something, then stand back to admire its *effect*.

3 **Disinterested** and **uninterested** – If you're disinterested, you are completely unbiased on a subject or issue. If you're uninterested, you couldn't care less about it.

4 **Dissect** and **bisect** – To dissect is to methodically cut apart, literally or figuratively. The more common 'bisect' means to cut in two, to split into two parts.

5 **May** and **might** – Use 'may' when there is a fairly good possibility of something happening: 'I *may* go to the pub tonight.' 'Might' suggests something is possible but far more remote: 'I *might* run a marathon.'

Hoard and **horde** – A hoard is a collection of items, often one that is carefully guarded. 'Horde' means a large group of people, be it a collection of football fans or an army of bloodthirsty warriors.

Reign and **rein** – 'Reign' refers to the rule of a monarch: 'the Queen *reigns* over the United Kingdom'. Reins are the thin straps used to control the movements of an animal or small child.

Whether and **if** – Only use 'whether' if you have two or more options: 'I don't know *whether* to have curry or pizza. Or some crisps.' Only ever use 'if' when you have no alternatives.

Loath and **loathe** – 'Loath' means to be reluctant or unwilling to do something. To loathe is to actively hate something or somebody.

Tortuous and **torturous** – Something tortuous is full of twists (for example, a story or an Alpine road). If it's torturous, it's particularly painful to endure.

10 questions on Britain you should be able to answer

1 Which two are civil war battles?
A. Waterloo **B.** Marston Moor **C.** Hastings **D.** Naseby

2 What are the names of the two main groups in Parliament in the early 18th century?

3 Why was Magna Carta important?
A. It gave all men the vote **B.** It limited the power of the monarch
C. It established a new system of education **D.** It gave women the vote

4 Which two types of cases are held in county courts?
A. Divorce **B.** Murder **C.** Minor criminal offences **D.** Breaches of contract

5 For approximately how long did the Romans stay in this country?
A. 50 years **B.** 100 years **C.** 400 years **D.** 600 years

6 What is Sake Dean Mahomet famous for?
A. Introducing tea-drinking and bungalows into Britain from India.
B. Introducing curry houses and shampooing into Britain from India

7 Which two are 20th century British discoveries or inventions?
A. Cloning a mammal **B.** Cash machines (ATMs) **C.** Mobile phones
D. Walkmans

8 The following statement is TRUE or FALSE?
St Helena is a Crown dependency.

9 Which two famous London buildings are built in the 19th century 'Gothic' style?
A. St Paul's Cathedral **B.** The Houses of Parliament **C.** St Pancras Station **D.** Buckingham Palace

10 Of what product did Britain produce over half the world's supply in the 19th century?
A. Cotton cloth **B.** Beer **C.** Cigarettes **D.** Rubber

Source: The Home Office

These ten questions are taken from the Home Office's 'Life in the UK Test', the examination now required for settlement ('indefinite leave to remain') in the UK or British citizenship. The answers are below – score anything less than five and you may need to pack your bags.

Answers

1. (B) Marston Moor (1644) and (D) Naseby (1645) were battles in the English Civil War and both were won by the Parliamentary armies.

2. From 1689 onwards there were two main groups in Parliament known as the Whigs and the Tories.

3. (B). King John was forced by his noblemen to agree to the Magna Carta, which restricted the power of the monarchy.

4. (A) and (D). County courts deal with civil matters such as divorce and family disputes and breaches of contract.

5. (C). The Romans ruled Britain for almost 400 years from AD 43–410

6. (B). Sake Dean Mahomet (1759-1851) introduced both the concept of curry houses and shampooing to Britain from India.

7. (A) and (B). In 1996, Ian Wilmot and Keith Campbell led a team that cloned a mammal for the first time. In the 1960s, James Goodfellow invented the cash machine.

8. False. St Helena is a British overseas territory and not a Crown dependency.

9. (B) and (C).

10. (A). In the 19th century, Britain produced half the world's supply of coal, iron and cotton cloth.

10 questions that could have won you a million*

1 Where would a cowboy wear his chaps? (For £2,000)
A. On his hands **B.** On his arms **C.** On his legs **D.** On his head

2 Which of these zodiac signs is not represented by an animal that grows horns? (For £4,000)
A. Taurus **B.** Capricorn **C.** Aries **D.** Aquarius

3 Sherpas and Gurkhas are native to which country? (For £8,000)
A. Ecuador **B.** Morocco **C.** Nepal **D.** Russia

4 Former British Prime Minister Tony Blair was born in which country? (For £16,000)
A. Northern Ireland **B.** Scotland **C.** England **D.** Wales

5 Whose autobiography has the title A Long Walk to Freedom? (For £32,000)
A. Ranulph Fiennes **B.** Nelson Mandela **C.** Mikhail Gorbachev **D.** Mother Teresa

6 Duffel coats are named after a town in which country? (For £64,000)
A. Germany **B.** Holland **C.** Belgium **D.** Austria

7 Complete this stage instruction in Shakespeare's The Winter's Tale: 'Exit, pursued by a ...' (For £125,000)
A. Dog **B.** Tiger **C.** Bear **D.** Clown

8 The young of which creature is known as a squab? (For £250,000)
A. Octopus **B.** Pigeon **C.** Salmon **D.** Horse

9 Who is the patron saint of Spain? (For £500,000)
A. St John **B.** St James **C.** St Peter **D.** St Benedict

10 Which king was married to Eleanor of Aquitaine? (For £1 million)
A. Henry I **B.** Henry V **C.** Henry II **D.** Richard I

*These are the final ten (of 15) questions of the first episode of British TV show *Who Wants To Be A Millionaire?* in which a contestant won the million-pound prize. The winner was Judith Keppel; the programme aired in November 2000. The answers are below.

Source: *Who Wants To Be A Millionaire?*, Victory Television

Answers

1. C

2. D

3. C

4. B

5. B

6. C

7. C

8. B

9. B

10. C

The 10 most dangerous countries in the world

COUNTRY	HOMICIDES* BY FIREARM PER 100,000 POPULATIO
1 **Honduras**	91.
2 **El Salvador**	70.
3 **Jamaica**	41.
4 **Belize**	3
5 **Guatemala**	38.
6 **Bahamas**	36.
7 **Colombia**	33.
8 **South Africa**	30.
9 **Trinidad and Tobago**	26
10 **Dominican Republic**	2
USA	4.
Scotland	1.
Northern Ireland	1.
England and Wales	

*International homicide is defined as unlawful death purposefully inflicted on another person

†Figures for 2011

Source: United Nations Office on Drugs and Crime

The 10 most dangerous US states

STATE	HOMICIDES BY FIREARM PER 100,000 POPULATION*
District of Columbia	12.46
Louisiana	10.16
Mississippi	7.46
South Carolina	5.41
Michigan	5.06
Maryland	4.7
Missouri	4.64
Arkansas	4.39
New York	4.12
Pennsylvania	3.97

*Figures for 2011
Source: FBI Uniform Crime Reports

CRIME & PUNISHMENT

10 notorious crime gangs

1 **The Cosa Nostra** – Sicilian mob formed in the 19th century, later spreading into the USA, the Cosa Nostra made their name in organized crime, operating with a strict code of silence – *omerta*. Still powerful to this day, and frequently killing police, prosecutors and politicians attempting to loosen the gang's grip.

2 **Hell's Angels** – Bearded biker gang that began in California in 1948 but has since spread far and wide. Split into chapters, American members must have no sex offences against children and own a US-made motorbike, preferably a Harley Davidson. Often fight and kill members from rival motorbike gangs.

3 **The Thompson Gang** – Brutal Glasgow crime family that ruled the city between the 1970s and 1990s, progressing from moneylending and debt collection to protection and drugs. Those who crossed them met a bloody end, in one case a victim was shot in the head and up the anus.

4 **The Medellín Cartel** – A collection of Colombian drug criminals operating out of the country's second biggest city. Ruthlessly murdered anyone who stood in the way of their very lucrative operation, which reportedly shipped $60 million worth of cocaine around the world a day.

5 **The Mungiki** – Operating in Nairobi's larger slums, the name translates as 'multitude', fittingly given the gang's ever-increasing numbers. Heavily into murder, mutilation, racketeering, intimidation and extortion, often all at once, the Mungiki are as brutal as any gang on this list, thinking nothing of hacking heads off to achieve their nefarious aims.

6 **The Yakuza** – Japanese crime families split into three, the biggest being the Yamaguchi Gumi from the city of Kobi. Heavily tattooed and adhering to strict rituals, the Yakuza control Japan's sex trade, run protection and blackmail rackets and exact swift and final retribution on those who stand in their way.

Jamaican Posse – Emerging from Jamaica in the 1960s, the posses settled in major British cities and rebranded themselves Yardies. They quickly spread their criminal tentacles into the drug trade, prostitution and illegal drinking and gambling clubs and are, as a rule, violent and trigger-happy. The dominant Shower Posse is so named for showering rivals with bullets.

The Aryan Brotherhood – Supposedly formed by an Irish-American biker gang in San Quentin jail in 1964, the Brotherhood graduated from a solely racist organization to become a major player in organized and very violent crime. Figures claim they account for just 1 per cent of the US prison population but are responsible for 18–21 per cent of all prison murders.

Mara Salvatrucha (MS-13) – According to the FBI, MS-13 is currently America's most violent gang, made up of refugees from the 1980s Salvadorian civil war. The gang arrived in Los Angeles and took hold. Their business is drugs, gun and human trafficking, extortion, kidnapping, contract killing and plain old murder, and business is booming. Showing they meant business, they kidnapped and killed the son of the Honduran president.

The 18th Street Gang – Considered by some to be even better organized than the well-organized MS-13, the 18th Street Gang tread a similar path – drug and gun trafficking, robbery, pimping, extortion, contract killing and murder – both premeditated and off the cuff. What began in Los Angeles has since stretched far beyond, with the gang thought to be operating across 37 US states and numerous countries overseas.

10 serial killers they never caught

❶ The Servant Girl Annihilator – On New Year's Eve 1884, a servant girl was found face down in the snow in Austin, Texas, bludgeoned and hacked to death with an axe. Seven further servants were killed in the same fashion, but the murders stopped as suddenly as they had begun.

❷ Jack the Ripper – The world's most famous 'cold case', the Ripper murdered mainly prostitutes (five confirmed, 13 others suspected) around the impoverished Whitechapel area of East London in 1888, usually mutilating their bodies. More than 200 suspects have been named, but the case remains unsolved.

❸ The Axe Man of New Orleans – Murdered at least eight people in New Orleans and the surrounding areas between May 1918 and October the following year, breaking into houses through the back door and attacking with an axe or straight razor. A fan of jazz who described himself as a 'non-human spirit', the murders stopped suddenly and he was never caught.

❹ The Phantom Killer – Stalking the residents of Texarkana, Texas, for four months of 1946, the Phantom killed five and injured three in attacks that came in the dead of night, being dubbed the 'Texarkana Moonlight Murders'. He struck wearing a sack over his head, usually three weeks apart, then suddenly stopped. The case remains unsolved.

❺ Jack the Stripper – Fingered for a spate of 'nude murders' in 1964 and 1965, Jack was inspired in his approach by Jack the Ripper, killing and dumping at least six prostitutes in the River Thames. From 7,000 initial suspects, Scotland Yard whittled it down to three names, though no one was ever convicted and the killing spree suddenly ceased.

The Zodiac Killer – San Francisco's most infamous serial killer, who murdered somewhere between seven and 37 victims between December 1968 and October 1969, taunting the press and police as he went about his business. The case remains unsolved but open.

The Monster of Florence – Striking 14 times between 1974 and 1985, the Monster of Florence shot dead seven couples who were having sex in cars around the Tuscan province. Despite the longest manhunt in Italian history and the convictions of four local men at various points, the case remains unsolved.

Bible John – A Bible-quoting serial killer in late 1960s Glasgow, 'Bible John' strangled three woman with their own stockings. All three were reported to be menstruating at the time, with pads or tampons left beside their murdered bodies. He was never known to strike again, and also never caught.

The Stoneman – India's most infamous serial killer is thought to have murdered 13 victims in Calcutta in 1989, each of them homeless and bludgeoned over the head with a stone. Police linked him to a similar spree that saw 12 homeless people killed in Bombay (now Mumbai) in 1985, but never caught their man.

Beer Man – Murdering seven times in South Mumbai between October 2006 and January 2007, Beer Man was so named for the beer bottle found beside the body of each of his victims. The prime suspect was jailed for the murders in 2008, but acquitted in 2009.

10 hapless criminals

1 According to *The Independent*, the self-defence of a bag-snatching New York hoodlum was undermined in 1999, when he turned to the key witness and asked: 'Did you get a good look at my face when I snatched your bag?'

2 In 1977, near Scarborough, North Yorkshire, a man robbed a shop of £157. His face was disguised by his motorbike helmet. Sadly, said helmet was emblazoned with his name in large letters across the front. He received 200 hours of community service.

3 In the USA in 2006, an armed robber walked into a fireworks shop in Lac du Flambeau, Wisconsin, intent on relieving it of its takings. To get the attention of the staff, the criminal mastermind fired off a warning shot, which resulted in a series of very colourful explosions, starting a fire which destroyed the entire shop. He was later arrested.

4 In October 2009, two men were apprehended by US police after reports they had tried to break into a flat in Carroll, Iowa. They were easy to track down: the 'masks' they wore to conceal their identities was simply marker pen scribbled crudely across their sorry faces.

5 In 1989, having been spotted attempting to break into a car, a pair of teenage Californian criminals then attempted to evade the police by climbing over a fence. It was a very big fence, and one that took them into San Quentin, one of the world's most secure prisons.

6 Before robbing a house in Somerset in 2011, a dozy criminal decided to consume 11 Valium tablets. These made him tired, a deep sleep ensued and the hopeless criminal was discovered by the owner in the conservatory, cradling a pile of her DVDs.

In what is possibly an apocryphal tale, an unnamed man walked into a convenience store in Colorado Springs, Colorado, and demanded all the cash, plus a bottle of Scotch for good measure. The cashier asked to see his ID, which the robber provided. Satisfied, the cashier then handed it back and the robber made good his escape. He was free for two hours before police picked him up at the address on his ID.

In January 2012, while robbing a branch of the Halifax in the City of London, one easily confused criminal demanded £700,000 from the cashier. Alas, instead of handing over his bag to be filled with swag, he handed over his gun, then panicked and ran when the security shutters came down.

Having robbed a house in Dartford, Kent, in 2008, the hapless criminal attempted to make good his escape through a window. And he would have got away, had his foot not become caught, leaving him dangling upside down. He was freed when the police arrived, then jailed for three years.

On trial for the armed robbery of an Oklahoma City convenience store in 1985, the criminal was doing a reasonable job defending himself, until the store manager testified that he was the guilty man. Riled, the defendant jumped up and shouted at the manager: 'I should have blown your f**king head off!', pausing, before adding, 'If I'd been the one that was there.' He got 30 years.

10 peculiar British events

1 **The Great Dorset Stinging Nettle Eating Competition** (Marshwoo Dorset) – An hour to eat as many stinging nettles as pain and common sense allow. The winner receives £100 and a nice trophy. Beer allowed. Encouraged even.

2 **Puck Fair** (Killorglin, Ireland) – One of Ireland's oldest and greatest festivals, in which a mountain goat is crowned king and reigns ove the town of Killorglin for three strange days.

3 **Yorkshire Pudding Boat Race** (Brawby, North Yorkshire) – Expect boats shaped like Yorkshire puddings, made from flour, eggs and water, and finished with a few coats of yacht varnish before being raced across Bob's Pond.

4 **Bog Snorkelling Championships** (Llanwrtyd Wells, Powys) – More than 200 competitors swim/crawl 55 m (60 yd) through a mud-befuddled Welsh bog.

5 **Shrovetide Football** (Ashbourne, Derbyshire) – An oversized football match between two unruly mobs, played on a 'pitch' with goals set 4.8 km (3 miles) apart. Dates back to Elizabethan times and often violent.

World Championship Snail 'Race' (Congham, Norfolk) – An annual epic in which the first snail to race from the centre of a circle to the edge and out wins some lettuce. There's also a barbecue, but this isn't France so the snails are safe.

World Gurning Championships (Egremont, Cumbria) – In which ugly, often toothless individuals battle to contort their faces into the most heinous shape imaginable while praying the wind doesn't change. Part of the annual Egremont Crab Fair.

World Black Pudding Throwing Championship (Ramsbottom, Lancashire) – Contestants lob these blood puddings at a number of Yorkshire pudding targets. He who knocks down the most prevails.

World Worm Charming Championships (Willaston, Cheshire) – Thirty minutes to 'charm' as many worms to the surface of the ground and into a bucket. Music can work, no digging, and water is considered a stimulant and so banned.

Cheese Rolling (Cooper's Hill, Gloucestershire) – An enduring classic: despite the high broken-limb count, competitors chase a cheese down a suicidally steep hill to see who reaches the finish line first. The cheese always wins.

Top 10 places at risk of alien invasion in the UK*

1 London

2 Scarborough, North Yorkshire

3 Salisbury Plain, Wiltshire/Hampshire

4 Stirling, Stirlingshire

5 Goonhilly, Cornwall

6 Aldermaston, Berkshire

7 Bude, Cornwall

8 Menwith Hill, North Yorkshire

9 Malvern, Worcestershire

10 RAF Rudole Manor, Somerset

*The Top 10 hotspots ranked by The UFO Investigation & Research Unit to promote the computer game *Inversion* (2012)

Source: www.namcobandaigames.com

London tops this list as it houses central government, vital communications and key transport links, as well as being home to a large chunk of the UK population – these aliens aren't stupid. Many of the other places on the list – particularly Scarborough and Salisbury Plain – are found close to important military and research bases.

Top 10 tallest structures in Britain*

BUILDING/LOCATION	YEAR COMPLETED	STOREYS	HEIGHT†
The Shard (London)	2013	87	308.5 m (1,012 ft)
Emley Moor Transmitter (Huddersfield, West Yorkshire)	1971	1	280 m (918.4 ft)
One Canada Square (London)	1991	50	235.1 m (771.13 ft)
Heron Tower (London)	2011	46	202.52 m (664.27 ft)
HSBC World Headquarters (London)	2002	45	199.5 m (654.36 ft)
Citigroup European Headquarters (London)	2002	45	199.5 m (654.36 ft)
Tower 42 (London)	1980	47	183 m (600.24 ft)
30 St Mary Axe (London)	2003	41	179.8 m (589.74 ft)
BT Telecom Tower (London)	1966	34	177 m (580.56 ft)
Broadgate Tower (London)	2008	35	164.3 m (538.9 ft)

*As at November 2013

†Height measured to architectural top

Source: www.skyscrapernews.com

10 bizarre British laws that stand to this day

1 **It is illegal to keep a pigsty in front of your house** – Unless it is obscured from view by a wall or a fence, according to the Town Police Clauses Act 1847, section 28.

2 **It is illegal to destroy or deface money** – Under the Currency and Banknotes Act 1928, it is an offence to deface a banknote by printing, stamping or writing on it, but not a crime to deliberately destroy it.

3 **It is illegal to enter the Houses of Parliament wearing a suit of armour** – The 1313 Statute Forbidding Bearing of Armour prevents Members of Parliament from wearing armour in the House.

4 **It is illegal to drive cows down the roadway without the permission of the Commissioner of Police** – According to the Metropolitan Streets Act 1867, it is an offence to drive cattle through the streets between 10 a.m. and 7 p.m., except with the Commissioner's prior permission.

5 **It is illegal to eat mute swan unless you're the queen of Great Britain** – Mute swans are protected under the Wildlife and Countryside Act 1981; anyone found guilty of killing one faces a £5,000 fine or up to six months in prison.

6 **It is illegal to carry a plank along a pavement** – An offence under section 54 of the Metropolitan Police Act 1839, which also lists other offences as flying kites, playing annoying games and sliding on ice or snow in the street.

It is illegal to import Polish potatoes into England – Under the terms of the Polish Potatoes (Notification) in England Order 2004, 'No person shall, in the course of business, import into England potatoes which he knows to be or has reasonable cause to suspect to be Polish potatoes.'

It is illegal to be drunk in charge of a horse – According to the Licensing Act 1872. This rule also applies to taking control of a carriage, cow or steam engine, or while in possession of a loaded firearm. Understandably so, really.

It is illegal to beat or shake any carpet or rug in any street, unless done before 8 a.m. – A bizarre offence under section 60 of the Metropolitan Police Act 1839, and in other districts under section 28 of the Town Police Clauses Act 1847.

It is illegal to be drunk in a pub – Worryingly, under section 12 of the Licensing Act 1872, 'every person found drunk... on any licensed premises, shall be liable to a penalty'. Luckily, as you might have noticed, this is rarely policed. Also, since 1839 it has been an offence under the Metropolitan Police Act for the keeper of a public house to permit drunkenness or disorderly conduct on the premises.

10 unfortunate British place names

1 **Twatt** (Orkney Islands, Scotland)

2 **Assloss** (Kilmarnock, Scotland)

3 **Dull** (Perthshire, Scotland) – twinned with Boring in the USA

4 **Muff** (County Donegal, Ireland)

5 **Golden Balls** (Oxfordshire, England)

6 **Ugley** (Essex, England)

7 **Crapstone** (Devon, England)

8 **Brokenwind** (Aberdeenshire, Scotland)

9 **Nether Wallop** (Hampshire, England)

10 **Shitterton** (Dorset, England)

Top 10 most expensive streets in the world*

STREET/LOCATION	PRICE CHANGE YEAR ON YEAR	AVERAGE PRICE PER SQUARE METRE†
Pollock's Path (The Peak, Hong Kong, China)	+10%	HK$930,670 (approx. £73,500)
Kensington Palace Gardens (London, UK)	+2%	approx. £69,900
Avenue Princesse Grace (Monaco)	+5%	€65,000 (approx. £52,700)
Boulevard du Général de Gaulle (Cap Ferrat, France)	-5%	€60,000 (approx. £48,400)
Paterson Hill (Singapore)	+6.5%	SGD$53,800 (approx. £26,000)
Chemin de Ruth (Geneva, Switzerland)	-5%	CHF 30,000 (approx. £22,600)
Romazzino Hill (Sardinia, Italy)	stable	€25,000 (approx. £20,000)
Ostozhenka (Moscow, Russia)	+3.6%	US$29,000 (approx. £18,000)
Fifth Avenue (New York City, USA)	+5.4%	US$28,000 (approx. £17,100)
Avenue Montaigne (Paris, France)	-3%	€20,000 (approx. £16,000)

*Ranking as at December 2013

†Pound sterling conversions correct as at December 2013

Source: Billionaire, www.billionaire.com

10 unexpected foreign place names

1 **No Name** (Colorado, USA)

2 **Boring** (Oregon, USA)

3 **Anus** (Burgundy, France)

4 **Fart** (Virginia, USA)

5 **Blowhard** (Victoria, Australia)

6 **Dildo** (Newfoundland, Canada)

7 **Lonelyville** (New York, USA)

8 **Fucking** (Tarsdorf, Austria)

9 **Hell** (Michigan, USA)

10 **Why** (Arizona, USA)

Top 10 largest British Overseas Territories*

OVERSEAS TERRITORY/LOCATION	AREA†
1 **The Falkland Islands** (South Atlantic Ocean)	12,000 sq km (4,700 sq miles)
2 **Turks and Caicos Islands** (Caribbean)	430 sq km (166 sq miles)
3 **Territory of St Helena, Ascension and Tristan da Cunha** (South Atlantic Ocean)	420 sq km (162 sq miles)
4 **Cayman Islands** (Caribbean)	260 sq km (100 sq miles)
5 **Sovereign Base Areas of Akrotiri and Dhekelia** (Cyprus, Mediterranean)	255 sq km (98.5 sq miles)
6 **British Virgin Islands** (Caribbean)	153 sq km (59 sq miles)
7 **Montserrat** (Caribbean)	102 sq km (39 sq miles)
8 **Anguilla** (Caribbean)	90 sq km (35 sq miles)
9 **Bermuda** (North Atlantic Ocean)	53 sq km (20.5 sq miles)
10 **Pitcairn Islands** (Pitcairn, Henderson, Ducie and Oeno, Pacific Ocean)	45 sq km (17 sq miles)

*With permanent populations

†All areas are approximate but as accurate as records allow

The remaining permanently inhabited British Overseas Territory is Gibraltar (Mediterranean, 6.5 sq km/2.5 sq miles). The other three BOTs – British Antarctic Territory (5,425,000 sq km/2,095,000 sq miles), the British Indian Ocean Territory (54,400 sq km/21,000 sq miles), and South Georgia and the South Sandwich Islands (South Atlantic Ocean, 3,903 sq km/1,500 sq miles) – do not have permanent populations.

10 barely inhabited islands

ISLAND/LOCATION	TERRITORY OF	AREA	INHABITANTS
1 **Tromelin** (Scattered Islands, Indian Ocean)	France	0.8 sq km (0.3 sq miles)	4
2 **Bear Island** (Svalbard, Arctic Ocean)	Norway	178 sq km (69 sq miles)	9
3 **Raoul Island** (Kermadec Islands, Pacific Ocean)	New Zealand	29.4 sq km (11.3 sq miles)	10
4 **Laurie Island** (South Orkney Islands, Antarctic Ocean)	Antarctica	86 sq km (33 sq miles)	14-45
5 **Macquarie Island** (Pacific Ocean)	Australia	128 sq km (49.5 sq miles)	20-40
6 **Amsterdam Island** (Indian Ocean)	France	58 sq km (22 sq miles)	25
7 **Possession Island** (Crozet Islands, Indian Ocean)	France	150 sq km (58 sq miles)	26-45
8 **Trindade and Martim Vaz** (South Atlantic Ocean)	Brazil	10 sq km (4 sq miles)	32
9 **Pitcairn Island** (Pacific Ocean)	UK	4.5 sq km (1.7 sq miles)	48
10 **Tristan da Cunha** (South Atlantic Ocean)	UK	104 sq km (40 sq miles)	264

*Populations may have altered slightly due to births, deaths, arrivals and departures

Source: Judith Schalanksy, *The Atlas of Remote Islands* (Penguin Books Ltd, 2010). Copyright © Judith Schalanksy, 2010

The 10 most destructive hurricanes in the USA*

HURRICANE/YEAR	LOCATION	CATEGORY†	ESTIMATED NUMBER KILLED
1 Great Galveston Hurricane (1900)	Texas	4	8,000
2 Lake Okeechobee Hurricane (1928)	Florida	4	2,500
3 Hurricane Katrina (2005)	Louisiana, Mississippi, Florida, Georgia, Alabama	3	1,200
4 Cheniere Caminada Hurricane (1893)	Louisiana	4	1,100–1,400
5 Sea Islands Hurricane (1893)	South Carolina, Georgia	3	1,000–2,000
6 Georgia and South Carolina Hurricane (1881)	Georgia, South Carolina	2	700
7 Hurricane Audrey (1957)	Louisiana, Texas	4	416
8 Great Labor Day Hurricane (1935)	Florida Keys	5	408
9 Last Island Hurricane (1856)	Louisiana	4	400
10 Miami Hurricane (1926)	Florida, Mississippi, Alabama, Pensacola	4	372

*Including contiguous USA but excluding Hawaii and Alaska

†Hurricane categories – 1: 119–153 km/h (74–95 mph); 2: 154–177 km/h (96–110 mph); 3: 178–209 km/h (111–130 mph); 4: 210–250 km/h (131–155 mph); 5: 251+ km/h (156+ mph)

Source: Weather Underground, www.wunderground.com

Top 10 tallest buildings in the world*

BUILDING/LOCATION	YEAR COMPLETED	STOREYS	HEIGHT
1 Burj Khalifa (Dubai, United Arab Emirates)	2010	163	828 m (2,716.5 ft)
2 Shanghai Tower (Shanghai, China)	2014	121	632 m (2,703 ft)
3 Makkah Royal Clock Tower Hotel (Abraj Al Bait) (Mecca, Saudi Arabia)	2012	120	601 m (1,972 ft)
4 One World Trade Center (New York, USA)	2014	104	541 m (1,776 ft)
5 Taipei 101 (Taipei, China)	2004	101	509 m (1,670 ft)
6 Shanghai World Financial Center (Shanghai, China)	2008	101	492 m (1,614 ft)
7 International Commerce Centre (Hong Kong, China)	2010	108	484 m (1,588 ft)
=8 Petronas Tower I (Kuala Lumpur, Malaysia)	1998	88	452 m (1,483 ft)
=8 Petronas Tower II (Kuala Lumpur, Malaysia)	1998	88	452 m (1,483 ft)
10 Zifeng Tower (Nanjing, China)	2010	66	450 m (1,476 ft)

*As ranked by Emporis as at December 2013, based on more than 400,000 buildings worldwide and including buildings that are either completed or have been topped out – i.e. have reached their final height. Buildings that are currently under construction, but have not yet reached their final height, are not included.

Source: Emporis, www.emporis.com

Top 10 most populated cities on the planet (now and in the future)

CITY/LOCATION	POPULATION (2011)	CITY/LOCATION	PREDICTED POPULATION (2025)
1 Tokyo (Japan)	37.2 million	**Tokyo** (Japan)	38.7 million
2 Delhi (India)	22.7 million	**Delhi** (India)	32.9 million
3 Mexico City (Mexico)	20.4 million	**Shanghai** (China)	28.4 million
3 New York-Newark (USA)	20.4 million	**Mumbai** (India)	26.6 million
5 Shanghai (China)	20.2 million	**Mexico City** (Mexico)	24.6 million
6 São Paulo (Brazil)	19.9 million	**New York-Newark** (USA)	23.6 million
7 Mumbai (India)	19.7 million	**São Paulo** (Brazil)	23.2 million
8 Beijing (China)	15.6 million	**Dhaka** (Bangladesh)	22.9 million
9 Dhaka (Bangladesh)	15.4 million	**Beijing** (China)	22.6 million
10 Calcutta (India)	14.4 million	**Karachi** (Pakistan)	20.2 million

Source: United Nations, Department of Economic and Social Affairs, Population Division (2012), 'World Urbanization Prospects, The 2011 Revision, Highlights', New York (ESA/P/WP/224)

London's 2011 population was put at 8.2 million by the Office for National Statistics (www.ons.gov.uk). By 2025, it is predicted it will have risen to 10.3 million, putting it 37th on the above list.

10 strange foreign festivals

❶ Baby-jumping Festival (Castrillo de Murcia, Burgos, Spain) –
At 'El Colacho', men dressed as devils leap over rows of confused
babies lying in the street.

❷ Wife-carrying World Championships (Sonkajärvi, Finland) – Men
run a race with their wives on their backs, with the victor's prize
being his wife's weight in beer.

❸ Frog Festival (Rayne, Louisiana, USA) – A celebration of the frog,
in the frog capital of the world. Races, rides and a chance to eat the
very thing you've turned up to celebrate.

❹ Naked Festival (Konomiya, Japan) – Or, in Japanese, 'Hadaka
Matsuri', in which participants dressed in loincloths throw water and
mud at each other to symbolize purification, or something.

❺ La Tomatina (Buñol, Valencia, Spain) – Participants, 20,000 and
more of them usually, lob over-ripe tomatoes at each other, either to
symbolize anti-Franco protests of the 1940s or more likely just for
the buzz of it.

The Redneck Games (East Dublin, Georgia, USA) – An alternative Olympics, featuring toilet-seat throwing, bobbing for pig's trotters and the mud pit belly flop. Mullet optional.

Moose Dropping Festival (Talkeetna, Alaska, USA) – A celebration of moose dung, in which – among other memorable events – men in hot air balloons drop bags of moose waste on the revellers below.

Roadkill Cook-off (Marlinton, West Virginia, USA) – A celebration of the critters scraped up off the road, cooked and served to a large number of like-minded celebrants.

Spam Jam (Waikiki, Hawaii, USA) – Hawaii is one of the largest consumers of Spam in the world, which is why 25,000 visitors to Waikiki engage in an annual celebration of the canned, spiced pork product.

The Testicle Festival (Clinton, Montana, USA) – An adults-only affair, featuring oil wrestling, wet T-shirt competitions and the consuming of 'Rocky Mountain oysters' – aka bull's cobblers.

10 alternative capitals of the world*

1 **Avon, Ohio (duct tape capital of the world)** – Home to the Duck-brand duct tape factory and the Avon Heritage Duct Tape Festival.

2 **Green Bay, Wisconsin (toilet paper capital of the world)** – The first splinter-free toilet paper was produced here, by Northern Paper Co.

3 **Fort Payne, Alabama (sock capital of the world)** – At one time, the socks worn by one in every eight Americans were made here, but production has declined.

4 **Mount Horeb, Wisconsin (mustard capital of the world)** – Home to the Mount Horeb Mustard Museum, where more than 3,500 are on show.

5 **La Crosse, Kansas (barbed wired capital of the world)** – Home to the Kansas Barbed Wire Museum, which itself is home to more than 2,000 types of barbed wire.

6 **Cordele, Georgia (watermelon capital of the world)** – Prolific producer of the fruit, and host to the annual Watermelon Days Festival.

7 **Martinsville, Indiana (goldfish capital of the world)** – Once home to the largest goldfish hatchery in the world, though production has waned in recent years.

8 **Strong, Maine (toothpick capital of the world)** – At its peak, the town was reportedly producing 20 million toothpicks a day. Production ceased in 2003 but the legend lives on.

9 **Sheboygan, Wisconsin (bratwurst capital of the world)** – Home to a two-day festival called Bratwurst Days, a celebration of the questionable pork product.

10 **Scottsboro, Alabama (lost luggage capital of the world)** – All of America's lost luggage ends up here, sold off to the public at knock down prices.

*Of course, we say 'world' but, clearly, they're all in the USA

Top 10 hottest and coldest places on the planet

LOCATION	TEMPERATURE*
1 Al'Aziziyah, Libya	57.8°C (136.04°F)
2 Death Valley, California, USA	56.7°C (134.06°F)
3 Ghudamis, Libya	55°C (131°F)
3 Kebili, Tunisia	55°C (131°F)
5 Timbuktu, Mali	54.5°C (130°F)
6 Snag, Yukon, Canada	-63°C (-81.4°F)
7 North Ice, Greenland	-66°C (-86.8°F)
8 Verkhoyansk, Russia	-69.8°C (-93.64°F)
9 Oymyakon, Russia	-71.2°C (-96.16°F)
10 Vostok Station, Antarctica	-89.2° C (-128.56°F)

*The highest/lowest recorded temperature at each location

Top 10 happiest countries in the world*

COUNTRY	'HAPPINESS' POINTS
1 **Denmark**	7.693
2 **Norway**	7.655
3 **Switzerland**	7.65
4 **Holland**	7.512
5 **Sweden**	7.48
6 **Canada**	7.47
7 **Finland**	7.389
8 **Austria**	7.369
9 **Iceland**	7.355
10 **Australia**	7.35

Notable others

13	*New Zealand*	7.22
17	*USA*	7.08
18	*Ireland*	7.076
22	*United Kingdom*	6.88

*2013 ranking

†Points are calculated based on a 156-nation survey covering seven topics including 'healthy life expectancy', 'social support', 'freedom to make life choices' and 'perceptions of corruption'

Source: 'World Happiness Report 2013', United Nations Sustainable Development Solutions Network, www.unsdsn.org

The 10 unhappiest countries in the world*

COUNTRY	'HAPPINESS' POINTS†
Togo	2.936
Benin	3.528
Central African Republic	3.623
Burundi	3.706
Rwanda	3.715
Tanzania	3.77
Guinea	3.847
Comoros	3.851
Syria	3.892
Senegal	3.959

*2013 ranking

†Points are calculated based on a 156-nation survey covering seven topics including 'healthy life expectancy', 'social support', 'freedom to make life choices' and 'perceptions of corruption'

Source: 'World Happiness Report 2013', United Nations Sustainable Development Solutions Network, www.unsdsn.org

HISTORY

10 rulers' gruesome deaths

1 King Adolf Frederick (gluttony) – The 18th-century Swedish monarch ate himself to death. After feasting on caviar, sauerkraut, smoked herring, lobster and champagne, he topped off with 14 *semlas* (sweet buns in hot milk). Unsurprisingly, the king developed intestinal problems and passed away.

2 King Edward II of England (killed with a hot rod) – Incompetent and pleasure-loving, Edward II met a nasty end. Tradition has it that he was murdered in 1327 by having a red-hot iron or copper rod inserted into his anus after being dethroned and imprisoned by his wife, Queen Isabella, and her lover, Roger Mortimer.

3 Sigurd the Mighty (death caused by a dead man's teeth) – The second Viking Earl of Orkney decapitated the head of his enemy Mael Brigte and attached it to his horse's saddle. However, the dead Brigte had his revenge when his teeth grazed against Sigurd's leg as he rode, causing a fatal septic infection that earned him a swift journey to Valhalla.

4 Richard III (death by angry mob) – It's bad enough ending up under a car park in Leicester, but the king suffered far worse at Bosworth in 1485. Betrayed by his kinsmen, he was surrounded, unhorsed and, despite fighting like a demon, was hacked and bludgeoned into the ground by the mob. His corpse was stripped naked, besmirched with filth and strapped to his horse before being put on public display.

5 King Edmund Ironside (stabbed bowels) – In 1016, 'having occasion to retire to the house for receiving the calls of nature, the son of the ealdorman Eadric, by his father's contrivance, concealed himself in the pit, and stabbed the king twice from beneath with a sharp dagger, and, leaving the weapon fixed in his bowels, made his escape'. At least, according to the account of Henry of Huntingdon.

King Herod the Great (genital gangrene) – The bloody ruler of ancient Judea died in 4 BC from a combination of chronic kidney disease and a rare infection that causes gangrene of the genitalia.

George, Duke of Clarence (drowned in wine) – The duke was convicted of treason against his brother King Edward IV and was allowed to choose his own death in the Tower of London. Tradition tells us that, being a heavy drinker, he opted to be drowned in a 'butt' (477 litres/105 imperial gallons) of Malmsey (Madeira) wine.

King Bela I of Hungary (crushed by a throne) – The king received news in 1063 that the Germans had invaded his country in support of deposed King Saloman. However, before he had a chance to confront his enemies, he was killed in his summer palace of Dömös after his throne toppled on him, crushing the unfortunate monarch.

Qin Shi Huang (poisoned by mercury) – China's first emperor thought he'd cracked the miracle of eternal life by taking a potion specially prepared by his court alchemists and physicians. Unfortunately, it was concocted from mercury and brought about his death.

Charles II of Navarre (death caused by a candle) – The disabled king was advised by his doctor to be wrapped from head to foot in brandy-soaked linen cloth to alleviate his pain. Unfortunately, the attendant sewing up the linen cut the thread with the flame of a candle, which immediately ignited the spirit-soaked and encased king and he was burnt to death in his palace.

10 excruciating torture devices

1 Thumbscrews – A simple but popular device that saw a wooden bar designed to apply pressure on the thumb when the screw was turned. Designed to coax out a confession rather than kill.

2 The rack – Infamously, the victim was tied down and as a wheel was cranked, the ropes holding them in place stretched them out until their limbs were torn off and death came as a blessed relief.

3 The Pear of Anguish – Stuck down the throat or up the back passage of a suspected homosexual or the front bottom of a suspected witch, the smooth pear featured a key which, once turned, opened out four metal leaves which caused terrible damage to the victim's innards.

4 Wheels – A simple conceit. Find a victim, tie them to a large wheel and then roll it down a rocky hill. Often, victims had their limbs broken and were left to hang out in the baking sun for days, draped over the wheel and attached to the top of a wooden pole.

5 The Brazen Bull – A large, hollow, brass statue of a standing bull, into which the victim was inserted. The door was shut, a fire started beneath the bull and the victim's desperate thrashings as he burned inside gave the impression the bull was alive.

6 The Iron Maiden – An iron cabinet large enough to accommodate an unfortunate victim. Smooth on the outside but spike-covered on the interior, once the door was closed on him those spikes would pierce his body and guarantee a long, slow, lingering death.

The Scavenger's Daughter – An A-frame-shaped metal rack on which the head was strapped to the top point of the A, the hands at the midpoint and the legs at the lower spread ends; swinging the head down and forcing the knees up in a sitting position so compressed the body as to force the blood from the nose and ears.

The head crusher – As advertised, a contraption that compressed around the skull at the turn of a screw, usually resulting in the victim's jaw shattering and his eyes exploding from his head. Often used to tease out a confession.

The hand saw – Popular in the Middle Ages for those suspected of adultery or blasphemy, this was literally a saw used to cut the victim in half, but with a twist. At the point the torturer reached the victim's abdomen, the victim was hung upside down and what blood remained flowed to their brain, keeping them conscious to lengthen the suffering.

The Guided Cradle – Imagine a pyramid-shaped chair, with the victim naked and sitting on the very point of said pyramid. The victim was slowly lowered on to the tip so that it bore violently up their anus. Also known as the Judas Cradle, and the Vigil.

10 surprising facts about Winston Churchill

1 **He was captured by Boer guerrillas** – During the Boer War, while working as a war correspondent, Churchill was taken as a prisoner of war before making a bold escape with other prisoners. His exploits earned him great fame and set him on the road to his political career.

2 **He was exactly twice his father's age when he died** – His father, Lord Randolph Churchill, died of syphilis on 24 January 1895, aged 45. Churchill passed away at 90, exactly 70 years to the day his father died.

3 **He was a member of the Tuna Club** – The oldest fishing club in southern California, USA; its members at one time also included Theodore Roosevelt, George S. Patton, Charlie Chaplin and Bing Crosby.

4 **He designed a boxed set of greetings cards for Hallmark** – Churchill met company founder J. C. Hall in 1946 and shortly afterwards Hall secured the rights to reproduce Churchill's paintings on greeting cards, which were published in the winter of 1950.

5 **His Parliament Square statue contains an electric current** – The 3.7 m (12 ft) bronze statue has an electric current running across the head to deter pigeons from sitting and defecating on the wartime leader.

He invented the onesie – Churchill wore what was called a siren suit, based on the boiler suits worn by the workmen at Chartwell. Posh Jermyn Street shirtmakers Turnbull & Asser made a variety of them for him, including a formal black one, a grey pinstripe and a red velvet.

He received colleagues while in the bath – The wartime leader, meeting ministers and officers while he was either in the bath or stepping out of it, referred to them as his Companions of the Bath. Secret Service Chief Brigadier Menzies described him as 'a nice pink pig wrapped in a silk kimono'.

He got drunk with Stalin – In 1942, Churchill and Russian leader Joseph Stalin were having difficulties over vital war talks in Moscow, until an eight-hour drinking binge lasting until 3 a.m. broke the ice.

He had gold-mounted false teeth – A partial set of these, designed to disguise Churchill's lisp, sold for £15,200 at auction in the UK in July 2010.

He relieved himself in the Rhine – When Churchill finally reached the Rhine in 1945, he ceremoniously unzipped his flies and with a 'childish grin of intense satisfaction' urinated in the river, fulfilling a long-held desire to display his contempt for Hitler and the Nazis.

10 surprising facts about Adolf Hitler

1 **He had a very sweet tooth** – Hitler consumed 900 g (2 lb) of chocolate, sweet pastries and hot chocolate every day. He drank tea with seven sugars. Unsurprisingly, he also had extreme dental decay and very bad breath.

2 **He had ambitions to become an artist** – Hitler, however, was rejected by the Academy of Fine Arts Vienna twice (in 1907 and 1908) and went to live in a homeless shelter. Many of his paintings are kept under lock and key by the US government.

3 **He plotted to kill Sir Winston Churchill with exploding chocolate** – The explosive devices were covered with a thin layer of dark chocolate and wrapped in expensive-looking black and gold paper branded 'Peter'. British spies and MI5 foiled the plot.

4 **He issued Nazi soldiers with blow-up sex dolls** – These were supposed to cut down on syphilis infections from French prostitute. The smaller-than-life-sized Aryan 'comforters' were designed to fit easily into a soldier's backpack. However, the embarrassed troops refused to carry them in case they were captured and their inflatab friends were found by enemies.

5 **His soldiers were high on speed when they invaded Poland and France** – Military doctors handed out Pervitin pills to troops, which contained the highly addictive Class A drug crystal meth. They also dosed chocolate with methamphetamine, giving *Fliegerschokolade* ('flyer's chocolate') to pilots. The speed sweet was given to tank crews, too, and dubbed *Panzerschokolade* ('tanker's chocolate').

He loved Hollywood movies – Hitler had his own private cinema, and enjoyed *King Kong* (1933), *Lives of a Bengal Lancer* (1935) and Charlie Chaplin films, but his favourite was Disney's *Snow White and the Seven Dwarves* (1937).

The Nazi rallying call was inspired by American football cheerleaders – '*Sieg Heil*!' was used by Hitler to rouse the crowds at his numerous rallies. Adolf Hitler was apparently a big fan of college football.

His doctor gave him bizarre cocktails of drugs – Nicknamed the 'Reich Injection Master', Hitler's personal doctor, Theodor Morell, was known to 'treat' the Führer with cocktails of drugs, vitamins and other substances. By April 1945, Hitler was taking 28 different pills, bi-hourly glucose injections, cocaine eye drops and a daily 'jab' of crystal meth.

He suffered from insomnia – Hitler would regularly stay awake until 4 or 5 a.m., constantly pacing the floor, always diagonally across the room, from corner to corner and whistling Walt Disney's 'Who's Afraid of the Big Bad Wolf?'

He suffered from stomach problems – Present from childhood, these caused 'uncontrollable flatulence', and he ate mainly raw vegetables. His doctor recorded in his diary that after Hitler downed a typical vegetable platter, 'constipation and colossal flatulence occurred on a scale I have seldom encountered before'. His generals must really have looked forward to their meetings.

10 legendary pirates

1 **Edward 'Blackbeard' Teach** – Pistol-packing English pirate who stormed ships in the West Indies and around the eastern coast of the American colonies with lit fuses blazing in his hair and beard – a look adopted by Keith Richards for Rolling Stones shows. Killed by a Royal Navy patrol at Ocracoke Inlet, North Carolina, he was beheaded but his body was thrown overboard and legend has it that it swam around the ship three times before sinking.

2 **Benito Soto Aboal** – Spanish pirate and one of the most bloodthirsty in history, murdering crews, sinking ships and raping women passengers. Met an appropriately violent end in Gibraltar in 1830, where he was hanged and his head stuck on a spike for public enjoyment.

3 **Grace O'Malley** – Pirate, trader and Irish clan chieftain who was also known as the 'Pirate Queen of Connaught', O'Malley plundered Turkish and Spanish pirates and even the English fleets to enrich her estate on Ireland's west coast. Her daring knew no bounds; she even travelled to the court of Elizabeth I to successfully negotiate the release of her family and assets with the Virgin Queen.

4 **Captain Kidd** – Poacher turned gamekeeper, the former 17th-century pirate hunter gained notoriety on the high seas by looting and plundering, before developing a guilt complex and returning to Blighty to clear his name. Not a good idea. He was jailed and hanged – allegedly to hide the identity of his secret financial backers.

5 **Captain Sir Admiral Henry Morgan** – One of the most successful and ruthless privateers ever to sail the Caribbean Sea. Knighted and appointed deputy governor of Jamaica by King Charles II, he retired to his sugar plantations on the island. And later had a bottle of rum named after him.

William Dampier – A contrary Englishman: on one hand a despised and villainous pirate who enjoyed plundering ships across the Atlantic and Pacific; on the other, one of the 17th century's most respected naturalists, celebrated author and the first man to circumnavigate the globe three times as well as mapping Australia.

Anne Bonny – The lover of Cuban-English pirate captain 'Calico' Jack Rackham, Bonny was also one of his most terrifying pirates. She had little sympathy for the hapless captain, for when Rackham was captured and sentenced to death, she allegedly said to him, 'If you had fought like a man, you need not have hanged like a dog.'

Henry 'Long Ben' Avery – Having mutinied on board a 17th-century ship of Englishmen fighting for Spain, he turned pirate and sailed halfway around the world capturing the treasure-packed ship of the Grand Mogul of India. Unlike most pirates, he managed to retire and enjoy his loot – his riches inspiring a whole generation of high seas villainy.

Barbarossa – Feared Barbary Coast pirate and admiral of the early 16th-century Ottoman fleet, named after his red beard. He terrorized Mediterranean countries, bringing death and destruction in his wake, and selling captives into Arab slavery. Such was his grip on North Africa that his pirate descendants were still ravaging the Mediterranean 300 years after his death.

François l'Olonnais – Bloodthirsty French pirate, once ripped out a captive's heart and gnawed on it before sailing to Cuba where he massacred the crew of a warship, leaving only one man alive to carry a message back to the governor. Karma came swiftly when l'Olonnais was captured, hacked to pieces, cooked over an open fire and eaten by cannibals somewhere in the Gulf of Darién.

10 of the bloodiest British battles

1 **Battle of Medway** – In AD 43, Roman invaders landed in Kent and overwhelmed and defeated the 150,000-strong British tribes, slaughtering at least 5,000 warriors in the process.

2 **Battle of Hastings** – In 1066, this battle saw as many as 100,000 killed (as claimed by Anglo-Norman chronicler Orderic Vitalis) or as 'few' as 6,000, according to more modern, revised figures.

3 **Battle of Stirling Bridge** – Around 5,000 English troops were left dead or wounded by William Wallace and Andrew Moray's joint Scottish forces at the Battle of Stirling Bridge in 1297.

4 **Battle of Bannockburn** – Robert Bruce's Scottish army routed the English at the Battle of Bannockburn in 1314, with an estimated 12,000 of opposing King Edward II's infantry and cavalry slain.

5 **Battle of Towton** – Fought in 1461, during the Wars of the Roses, this battle is considered the largest and bloodiest ever to take place on English soil, leaving an estimated 28,000 dead.

6 **Battle of Bosworth Field** – Plantagenet King Richard III lost 1,000 men-at-arms and his own life at the Battle of Bosworth Field in 1485, resulting in a bloody victory for Henry Tudor.

7 **Battle of Marston Moor** – This English Civil War battle near York in 1644 is one of the biggest battles ever staged on English soil and left some 4,300 dead – most of them Royalists.

8 **Battle of Naseby** – In 1645, during this key battle of the English Civil War, an estimated 5,000 men were slain as Cromwell's New Model Army defeated the Royalists.

9 **Battle of Culloden** – In 1746, the last pitched battle on British soil ended the Jacobite rebellion and left around 1,000 Jacobites and 300 government forces dead.

10 **Battle of Britain** – In 1940, the first major campaign to be fought entirely by air forces in UK airspace, and a decisive victory for the Allies, saw them lose 544 men, but the Germans lost over 2,500.

The figures quoted are as accurate as records allow.

Top 10 oldest London members' clubs

CLUB/LOCATION	FOUNDED
White's* (37 St James's Street, SW1)	1693
Boodle's* (28 St James's Street, SW1)	1762
Brooks's* (St James's Street, SW1)	1764
The Royal Thames Yacht Club† (60 Knightsbridge, SW1)	1775
The Travellers Club* (106 Pall Mall, SW1)	1819
The Oriental Club‡ (Stratford Place, W1)	1824
The Athenaeum† (107 Pall Mall, SW1)	1824
The Garrick Club* (15 Garrick Street, WC2)	1831
The City of London Club* (19 Broad Street, EC2)	1832
The Carlton Club† (69 St James's Street, SW1)	1832

*Male only
†Mixed membership
‡Women allowed associate membership only

10 unconventional fragrances

1 **Eau de funeral home** – Mixing lilies, carnations, gladioli and chrysanthemums with a dash of mahogany and a sniff of carpet, in 'Funeral Home', Demeter has created this classic stench of death.

2 **Eau de Stilton cheese** – Recreating 'the earthy and fruity aroma' of the stinking blue cheese, Eau de Stilton is 'an eminently wearable perfume'. Commissioned by the Stilton Cheesemakers' Association but sadly no longer on the market.

3 **Eau de hamburger** – Only in America, alas, but the Burger King-commissioned 'Flame' allowed fans of fast food to smell like beef, delivering 'the scent of seduction' with just a tasteful 'hint of flame broiled meat'.

4 **Eau de money** – Smell like a million dollars with his and hers 'Money', a fragrance combining 'the clean essence of cotton, linen and silk' with 'the formula used to make actual money'. To define your success, they claim, you must first smell like it.

5 **Eau de prostitute** – Black Phoenix Alchemy Lab's 'Bordello' perfume oil is said to evoke 'images of velvet-lined Old West cathouses, tightly laced corsets, rustling petticoats and coquettish snarls of pleasure'. Why not treat the wife or girlfriend?

Eau de blood, sweat, semen and spit – 'Secretions Magnifique' from Etat Libre d'Orange is supposedly 'an ode to the pinnacle of sexual pleasure, that extraordinary moment when desire triumphs over reason'.

Eau de whisky – Keen to smell like a drunkard? Then you need 'Double Whisky', the essential new fragrance from pioneering French fragrance house Evaflor.

Eau de cigarette smoke – Another classic from the creative minds at Etat Libre d'Orange, the 'Jasmin et Cigarette' is precisely that: a blend of a shrub mixed with the unmistakable stench of fags.

Eau de barbecue – That must-have whiff of smoke and burning meat, 'Que' (from the renowned perfume house Pork Barrel BBQ) delivers an 'intoxicating bouquet of spices, smoke, meat, and sweet summer sweat'.

Eau de vagina – Natural Vaginal Perfume Fragrance, brought to you, for reasons still unclear, by Vulva Original. No really, you shouldn't have.

10 notable conspiracy theories

1 **Colonel Gaddafi stole the racehorse Shergar** – Or rather, it was claimed that the former Libyan leader had the IRA steal the world's greatest racehorse of the time for him, in return for a large cache of weapons.

2 **NASA allegedly faked the moon landings in the 1960s** – The flag planted by Armstrong and Aldrin was blowing in the wind, despite there being no wind on the moon. There were also no stars visible and the shadows fell at strange angles. They claimed the USA faked the landing to get ahead of the USSR in the Space Race.

3 **Global warming is allegedly a myth** – Global temperatures have actually fallen; talk of warming is just a conspiracy to increase taxes and control lifestyles.

4 **Elvis Presley faked his own death** – The King didn't die on the toilet in 1977 (see page 118), it is claimed that he simply went into hiding and remained alive until the mid-1990s, finally dying in a motorcycle accident.

5 **Paul McCartney died in 1966** – Macca allegedly died in a car crash and was replaced by a look- and sound-a-like. As evidence of this, some claim that played backwards, the Beatles song 'Revolution 9' supposedly contains the line: 'Turn me on dead man, turn me on dead man' (see page 58).

6 **The September 11 attacks on the USA were allowed to happen** – It's been claimed that, despite warnings of the attack, America was happy to have a pretext to launch wars in the Middle East – and there was no way two planes could have brought the Twin Towers to the ground.

Tap water is designed to keep you in line – Adding fluoride to the water is not done to prevent tooth decay, as they'd have us believe. Rather, it is allegedly part of a New World Order (see No. 9) plot to take over the world – fluoride sterilizes humans and forces us into a state of calm compliance.

The AIDS virus was concocted in a laboratory – It's been claimed it was carefully cooked up in 1974 by the CIA or KGB as a way of controlling world population, particularly in expanding Africa. They have the cure but won't release it any time soon.

The whole world is allegedly controlled by less than 3,000 elite – The Illuminati and Bilderberg Group are part of a secretive New World Order who seek to rule the planet through a one-world government. It's claimed this power-crazed minority control every element of our lives.

The people in power are not human – Former BBC pundit David Icke claims that the people in positions of power are in reality blood-sucking, shape-shifting reptiles. And he includes the royal family among them.

10 unusual phobias

1 **Arachibutyrophobia** – The fear of peanut butter sticking to the roof of one's mouth

2 **Venustaphobia** – The fear of beautiful women

3 **Coprastasophobia** – The fear of becoming constipated

4 **Ergophobia** – The fear of work

5 **Lachanophobia** – The fear of vegetables

6 **Peladophobia** – The fear of bald people

7 **Syngenesophobia** – The fear of all relatives

8 **Pogonophobia** – The fear of beards

9 **Hippopotomonstrosesquippedaliophobia** – The fear of long word

10 **Phobophobia** – The fear of fear of a phobia

10 strange places the image of Jesus has been spotted

- **On a fish finger** (Kingston, Ontario, Canada) – April 2011

- **On a patch of damp behind a fridge** (Herne Bay, Kent, England) – October 2012

- **In a chicken's feathers** (Rowley Regis, West Midlands, England) – July 2010

- **On a Walmart receipt** (Anderson City, South Carolina, USA) – July 2011

- **On a toilet door at Ikea** (Glasgow, Scotland) – October 2009

- **On a naan bread** (Esher, Surrey, England) – January 2010

- **On the wall of a Chinese takeaway** (Sunderland, Tyne and Wear, England) – June 2012

- **On a bruise on a woman's arm** (Florida, USA) – 2010

- **On the top from a Marmite jar** (Rhondda, South Wales) – 2009

- **In a dog's bum hole** (Los Angeles, California, USA) – July 2006

10 cheap but mildly amusing *Carry On* characters

CHARACTER	FILM/YEA
1 Private Jimmy Widdle	*Carry On Laughing* (1981
2 Sergeant Ernie Knocker	*Follow That Camel* (1967
3 Sidney Fiddler	*Carry On Girls* (1973
4 Augusta Prodworthy	*Carry On Girls* (1973
5 Miss Bangor	*Carry On Girls* (1973
6 Cora Flange	*Carry On Abroad* (1972
7 Sergeant Jock Strapp	*Carry On Dick* (1974
8 Lord Peter Flimsy	*Carry On Laughing* (1975
9 Arthur Upmore	*Carry On Behind* (1975
10 Sir Roger Daley	*Carry On Dick* (1974

10 price hikes of popular consumer goods

YEAR	AVERAGE PRICE OF BEER*	AVERAGE PRICE OF CIGARETTES†	AVERAGE PRICE OF PETROL‡
1994	£1.58	£2.41	£0.51
1996	£1.73	£2.73	£0.56
1998	£1.89	£3.19	£0.65
2000	£2.00	£3.91	£0.80
2002	£2.09	£4.14	£0.74
2004	£2.33	£4.39	£0.80
2006	£2.51	£4.76	£0.91
2008	£2.74	£5.31	£1.07
2010	£2.94	£5.86	£1.17
2012	£3.18	£7.10	£1.36
Aug 2013	£3.30	£7.79	£1.37

*Per pint of draught lager

†For 20 king-size filter cigarettes

‡Per litre of unleaded petrol

Source: The Office of National Statistics, www.ons.gov.uk

10 weird theme parks

① Napoleonland (Paris, France) – Not yet built but expected in 2014, Napoleonland pays homage to the French leader/dictator with a recreation of Louis XVI on the guillotine, a water show depicting the Battle of Trafalgar and a ski slope littered with the frozen bodies of the perished. Fun for all the family.

② Dollywood (Pigeon Forge, Tennessee, USA) – This shrine to country music and the titular Miss Parton features more than 40 rides, including six rollercoasters. Sadly, none of them is in the shape of Dolly Parton but the place still pulls in more than 2.5 million visitors every year.

③ Hacienda Nápoles (Puerto Triunfo, Antioquia, Colombia) – Some 50,000 visitors are drawn annually to the Hacienda Nápoles theme park, built in the grounds of infamous drug lord Pablo Escobar's ranch. Expect full-size dinosaur sculptures, vintage cars, a swimming pool, zoo and an animal park, and an archway built from the plane he reportedly used to ship his first batch of cocaine into the USA.

④ Diggerland (Cullompton, Devon, UK) – One of four Diggerland theme parks dotted around Britain (the other three are located in Kent, Durham and Yorkshire), each offering a very hands-on celebration of diggers and JCBs. Expect digger-themed rides, high-octane digger racing and a sense of mild bemusement.

⑤ Dickens World (Chatham Dockyard, Kent, England) – Since 2007, this massive warehouse in Chatham Dockyard has played host to a fun-filled homage to the author of searing exposés of Victorian filth and human misery as depicted in such classics as *A Christmas Carol* and *The Adventures of Oliver Twist*. It houses, among other things, a *Great Expectations* boat ride through recreated London sewers, and Fagin's Den, a playground named after the villainous old scrote in *Oliver Twist*. Beware pickpockets, obviously.

Kingdom of the Little People (Kunming, China) – A charming Lilliputian land of little people or an insensitive joke at the expense of dwarves? It's a fine line. The employees here are all less than 1.3 m (4 ft 3 in) tall. They dance, sing and act out fairy tales for the amusement of the mainly full-sized visitors.

Holy Land Experience (Orlando, Florida, USA) – The centrepiece of an educational romp at this Christian theme park is the live crucifixion of 'Jesus Christ' – a man dressed to look like the Son of God, wailing loudly and doused in blood.

Grūtas Park (Druskininkai, Lithuania) – Aka Stalin World, which sounds even more spirit-crushingly bleak than Grūtas Park, this is a 200-hectare (500-acre) celebration of Lithuania gaining its independence, complete with watchtowers and barbed-wire fencing. Head here if Soviet-era sculptures, a Soviet-era playground and Soviet-era food in the Soviet-era restaurant are your thing. Oh, and there's also a zoo.

Osama bin Laden Land (Abbottabad, Pakistan) – That's not its real name, nor does it even exist – but it soon will. Plans are afoot to turn the compound in which the world's most wanted terrorist lived and died into a $30 million amusement park, with a zoo, water sports and rock climbing. It's probably not what he would have wanted.

Love Land (Jeju Island, South Korea) – One of the few theme parks not aimed at children. This erotic theme park is an adults-only affair and boasts 140 sculptures of people engaged in all manner of smutty positions, some of which are apparently interactive. Leave your inhibitions at the gate and be careful what you sit down on.

10 increasingly large numbers that follow one million

1 **Billion** – 1,000,000,000 (10^9)

2 **Trillion** – 1,000,000,000,000 (10^{12})

3 **Quadrillion** – 1,000,000,000,000,000 (10^{15})

4 **Quintillion** – 1,000,000,000,000,000,000 (10^{18})

5 **Sextillion** – 1,000,000,000,000,000,000,000 (10^{21})

6 **Septillion** – 1,000,000,000,000,000,000,000,000 (10^{24})

7 **Octillion** – 1,000,000,000,000,000,000,000,000,000 (10^{27})

8 **Nonillion** – 1,000,000,000,000,000,000,000,000,000,000 (10^{30})

9 **Decillion** – 1,000,000,000,000,000,000,000,000,000,000,000 (10^{33})

10 **Centillion** – 1,000,000,000,000,000,000,000,000,000,000,0
00,000,000,000,000,000,000,000,000,000,000,000,000,0
0,000,000,000,000,000,000,000,000,000,000,000,000,00
,000,000,000,000,000,000,000,000,000,000,000,000,000,
000,000,000,000,000,000,000,000,000,000,000,000,000,
00,000,000,000,000,000,000,000,000,000,000,000,000,0
0,000,000,000,000,000,000,000,000,000,000,000,000,00
,000,000,000,000 (10^{303})

These are numbers in the UK's preferred Short Scale number naming system, using numbers in formal mathematical use.

10 types of cloud*

1 **Cirrus** – high level

2 **Cirrocumulus** – high level

3 **Cirrostratus** – high level

4 **Altocumulus** – mid level

5 **Altostratus** – mid level

6 **Nimbostratus** – mid level

7 **Stratocumulus** – low level

8 **Stratus** – low level

9 **Cumulus** – low level

10 **Cumulonimbus** – low level

*The ten types of cloud are broken down into three categories: high level (above 6,000 m/20,000 ft); mid level (between 2,000–6,000 m/ 6,500–20,000 ft); and low level (below 2,000 m/6,500 ft).

Source: The Met Office, www.metoffice.gov.uk

Cumulonimbus is the bugger that will deliver and drop rain, snow and hail on your head, though not always all three at the same time. It is a heavy, dense, large cloud with a very dark, angry base. Its showers are often short but heavy, and if thunder and lightning occur, they'll be accompanied by cumulonimbus.

10 terms for killing

1 **Omnicide** – The act of killing all humans, to wipe out the human species

2 **Xenocide** – The act of killing an entire alien species

3 **Giganticide** – The act of killing a giant

4 **Regicide** – The act of killing a king

5 **Tyrannicide** – The act of killing a tyrant

6 **Dominicide** – The act of killing one's master

7 **Famacide** – The killing of another person's reputation

8 **Muscicide** – A concoction that kills flies

9 **Deicide** – The act of killing a god, goddess or divine being

10 **Chronocide** – The killing (or wasting) of time

10 bizarre patron saints

1 Saint Appolonia – The patron saint of dentists

2 Saint Ambrose – The patron saint of beekeepers

3 Saint Cajetan – The patron saint of the unemployed

4 Saint Joseph of Cupertino – The patron saint of air travellers, astronauts and pilots

5 Saint Genesius – The patron saint of clowns

6 Saint Drogo – The patron saint of unattractive people

7 Saint Malo – The patron saint of pigkeepers

8 Saint Bibiana – The patron saint of the hung over

9 Saint Roch – The patron saint of grave diggers

10 Saint Fiacre – The patron saint of haemorrhoid sufferers

By definition, a saint is believed to protect a particular place or type of person, supposedly bringing them better luck than they may have otherwise enjoyed.

10 odd superstitions

1 In Russia, whistling in the home is considered to invite in bad luck – the noise supposedly frightens away guardian angels.

2 Superstition dictates that many US hotels have no 13th floor or room 13. In China and Japan, the fourth floor will be missing – because the word for 'four' sounds like 'death' in both languages.

3 Many chefs insist on presenting an odd number of elements on the plate – this is said to relate to a Japanese superstition, although naysayers claim it just looks more presentable.

4 In Spain, at midnight on New Year's Eve, the superstitious eat 12 grapes – they symbolize the 12 months of the coming year and bring luck.

5 In India, some consider it bad luck to get their hair – head or facial – cut on a Tuesday. This is apparently down to astrology and the belief that a human's strength is stored in their hair.

6 In Russia, if a bird drops a poo on any part of you, your car or your property, it supposedly brings good luck and financial reward.

7 In England, some particularly nervous sorts believe that accidentally dropping an umbrella on the floor means that there will be a murder in the house.

8 In Japan, if you walk past a graveyard or a hearse passes you by, you must conceal your thumbs. In Japanese, 'thumb' translates as 'parent finger', so by concealing them you are protecting your parents.

9 In certain parts of Turkey, some believe that if you're chewing gum at night, you're chewing the flesh of the dead.

10 In Iceland, it is forbidden to knit on the doorstep in late winter, as the act is said to lengthen the duration of winter.

The 10 Commandments – a reminder

1 Thou shalt have no other gods.

2 Thou shalt not make any graven images.

3 Thou shalt not take the Lord's name in vain.

4 Remember the Sabbath day.

5 Honour thy father and mother.

6 Thou shalt not kill.

7 Though shalt not commit adultery.

8 Thou shalt not steal.

9 Thou shalt not bear false witness against thy neighbour.

0 Thou shalt not covet (anything that is your neighbour's).

10 dates for the end of the world

1 **1 February 1524** – As predicted by London astrologers, interpreting the alignment of planets in the (fishy) constellation Pisces to mean the world would be wiped out in a massive flood. Widespread panic ensued, for no good reason as it turned out.

2 **Between 1793 and 1795** – As predicted by the self-proclaimed 'Prince of the Hebrews', a retired Canadian sailor named Richard Brothers who couldn't be more specific than sometime between these two years. He was committed to an insane asylum in 1795.

3 **1806** – As predicted by 'The Prophet Hen of Leeds', who laid eggs on which the warning 'Christ is coming' was etched. It turned out to be a hoax – the words written on the eggs, which were then shoved back up the poor bird.

4 **20 May 1910** – As predicted by an astronomer claiming Earth would pass through the tail of Halley's Comet, which contained the poisonous gas cyanogen. A panicked public bought anti-comet pills and while Earth did pass through the comet, the world definitely didn't end.

5 **17 December 1919** – As predicted by seismologist and meteorologist Albert Porta, who predicted impending doom caused by the rare alignment of six planets that would create a huge magnetic current and cause the Sun to explode. That in turn would engulf the Earth and it would be curtains. Or so he said.

6 **1936** (and then 1943, 1972 and 1975) – As predicted by the Worldwide Church of God founder Herbert W. Armstrong, who warned that 'the Rapture' would arrive in 1936 and only members of his church would be saved. When it failed to materialize, he amended the prediction a number of times before giving up.

7 **10 March 1982** – As predicted in the book *The Jupiter Effect*, nine planets were set to align on the same side of the Sun with catastrophic, world-ending consequences on 10 March 1982. When that didn't happen, a follow-up, *The Jupiter Effect Reconsidered*, was rushed to print, but that didn't sell so well.

8 **21 May 1988** (and then 1992, 1994 and 2011) – As predicted by Californian Christian radio broadcaster Harold Camping, who, when proven wrong, revised the date to 15 September 1992, then 27 September 1992, then 2 October 1992, 7 September 1994, 21 May 2011 and 21 October 2011... he was widely ridiculed.

9 **21 December 2012** – According to an ancient Mayan prophecy, this was the day Earth would be in exact alignment with the Sun at the centre of the Milky Way galaxy, causing earthquakes, tsunamis and global change so significant it would spell curtains for Earth. But it didn't happen.

0 **Some time in 3240** – According to believers of Talmud and mainstream Orthodox Judaism, in a vision called the Messianic Prophecies, the Messiah will return 6,000 years after the creation of Adam (2240) and the Earth could end 1,000 years later. So consider that a vague date for your diary.

Acknowledgements

ACKNOWLEDGEMENTS

Dr Leon Foster
Juliet Gardner
Keir Radnedge
Mark Haupt
Martin Vacher
Matt Mason
Rick Archbold
Rob Orchard
Ryan Chambers

24/7 Wall St.
Airports Council International
Alexa
Autosaur
Best Ever Albums
Billionaire
Black Hills Reptile Gardens
Boxing News
Business Balls
CarLoan4U
Cycling Challenge
Death By Films
Delayed Gratification magazine
Emporis
Engineering Sport
FHM magazine
Genes Reunited
Golf World magazine
Honest John
Imperial War Museum
Institute For Plastination
Internet Movie Database

ACKNOWLEDGEMENTS

Kelkoo
Lovehoney
Mandatory
McDonald's
Medals Per Capita: Olympic Glory In Proportion
Men's Health magazine
Metacritic
Namco Bandai Games
National Eating Out Week
Organization For Economic Co-operation and Development
Outdoor Fitness magazine
Penguin Books
PepsiCo
Rate Your Music
Real Clear Sports
ResearchGate
Restaurant magazine
Road Safety Foundation
Rugby World
Sky Scraper News
Sponsorship Intelligence
Sport magazine
Sporting Intelligence
Sports Reference
Spotify
Stuff magazine
Sunday Sport
The Bookseller
The British Sandwich Association
The Co-operative
The Daft Name Directory
The Dinosaur Museum
The Drinks Business

ACKNOWLEDGEMENTS

The Drum
The Federal Bureau of Investigation
The Home Office
The Met Office
The Office For National Statistics
The Public Lending Right
The Royal College Of Midwives
The Royal Society For The Protection Of Birds
The Smoking Gun
Top Trumps
Total Film magazine
United Nations
VGChartz
Victory Television
Writers Guild Of America
Weather Underground
Wisden Cricketers' Almanack
YouTube Trends
ZenithOptimedia